The Spokesman
Speak Truth to Power
Edited by Ken Coates
Published by Spokesman for the Bertrand Russell Peace Foundation

Spokesman 79   2003

CONTENTS

Editorial	3	
Will Iran Be Next?	5	*Ken Coates*
Iraq, the United States and the End of the European Coalition	11	*Gabriel Kolko*
Who Rules the Peace when the Rulers Break the Rules?	21	*Phyllis Bennis*
The War on Freedom and Democracy	32	*Tony Bunyan*
On Twain, Lincoln, Imperialist Wars and the Weather	45	*Kurt Vonnegut*
Raiders of the Lost Iraq	49	*Robert Fisk*
The Price of Oil	56	*Zhores A. Medvedev*
Christopher Hill – A Man with a Mission	60	*V.G. Kiernan*
Peace Dossier	64	*'Warmongers Sell War'* *Parthenon Marbles* *Depleted Uranium* *UN in the Melting Pot...* *...and NATO as well?*
Reviews	75	*Ken Coates* *G. Allen* *Henry McCubbin*

Printed by the Russell Press Ltd., Nottingham, UK

ISSN 0262 7922   ISBN 0 85124 681 8

Subscriptions
Institutions £30.00/€60/$60
Individuals £20.00 (UK)
£25.00 (ex UK)
€40/$40

Back issues available on request

A CIP catalogue record for this book is available from the British Library

Published by the
Bertrand Russell Peace Foundation Ltd.,
Russell House
Bulwell Lane
Nottingham NG6 0BT
England
Tel. 0115 9784504
email:
elfeuro@compuserve.com
www.spokesmanbooks.com
www.russfound.org

Editorial Board:
Michael Barratt Brown
Ken Coates
John Daniels
Ken Fleet
Stuart Holland
Tony Simpson

Let's work for peace and human rights together

BILL MORRIS
General Secretary

TONY WOODLEY
General Secretary (Elect)

tel: 020 7611 2500
fax: 020 7611 2555

For further information visit our website
www.tgwu.org.uk

Transport and General Workers' Union

Editorial
Speak Truth to Power

At the end of June 2003, the European Network for Peace and Human Rights held its conference in the European Parliament. The horrors of the war on Iraq were by no means finished, but already there was deep disquiet about the possibility of continuing hostilities, and extending them to Iran, not to say Korea and other places far away from the Iraqi border.

Continued war, and continuing threats of war, persuaded the peace movements and their associates in the movement for human rights that they should make strenuous efforts to join their forces, bringing together not only movements in Europe and now, since the Cordoba conference, in the Middle East, but also seeking the opinions of American co-thinkers. So it was agreed to try to organise a meeting of the Network in the United States, possibly in Washington, under the heading 'Speak Truth to Power'. Peace people in the United States have been trying to do this for long enough: but it is arguable that Europeans can no longer achieve this objective within the continent of Europe alone, because the power that used to inhere in their own institutions has been to some degree displaced.

Concern about American military doctrines, notably that of Full Spectrum Dominance, reinforce the view that power has migrated across the Atlantic. As Gabriel Kolko argues below, this is an exaggeration, even if it is an understandable one. But nonetheless, the recovery of democracy, in Europe as in the United States, is a labour necessarily undertaken co-operatively.

During the British Foreign Secretary's visits to Baghdad, in a timorous hit and run mission, (in which, far from ceremonial parades and guards of honour, he was smuggled aboard a helicopter and hidden from view) it has been announced that the occupation of Iraq will take a very long time. Around the world, clients are drilled to provide levies of troops. There is public speculation about whether the occupation will continue for seven years or for ten. Sanitized, the public story is given out that it will last for two.

All of us can see how much worse this situation will become when the failure to create democratic institutions in Iraq becomes an object of anger among the people. Is it at that point that the crisis will be compounded by the invasion of Iran? And how will George Bush and Tony Blair administer the resultant convulsive mess? It might be possible to kill a large number of Iranians, and to augment the numbers of dead Iraqis. There can be a pogrom of the Ayatollahs. But peace? Nothing is less likely.

By far the best solution for this wholly unnecessary conflict, before it becomes a conflagration, is the withdrawal of the allied occupation. All of the international institutions which might have been helpful in securing this have incurred serious disabilities in the run up to the invasion: certainly the new American alliance, the stunningly mistitled 'Global Peacekeeping Force', is highly unlikely to substitute for either the UN, or even Nato.

Editorial

The UN Security Council was sabotaged by the United States, because it could not be induced to vote support for the American invasion of Iraq. The UN has been far from a free-standing agency for the upholding of justice: subject as it has been to great power manipulations of various kinds, not excluding outright bribery. But neither the wiles nor the chequebooks of American power could legitimate the proposed invasion.

Nato by contrast could not be relied upon for the invasion, because it is formally speaking an alliance, and its Council not only might disagree, but does disagree with the senior partner. American generals apparently decided as long ago as the Kosovo war that such an alliance was dysfunctional for actual fighting, since the subaltern members had a regrettable tendency to answer back, and to threaten disobedience.

The new proposal, reported in the *Los Angeles Times*, is to arrange for a standing international peacekeeping force which can be sent anywhere, without involving untoward arguments with American power. Such a force will indeed be necessary for a decade long occupation of Iraq, even if this does not turn into a simultaneous occupation of Iran. But where is it to be recruited? There are numerous client states, in various stages of dependency, and some have already been approached for a short-term occupation of Iraq by the British accomplice. But who will volunteer for the longer task, which will include the permanent occupation of all those other lawless territories, across Central Asia, and out to the Korean periphery? Perhaps the various missions to Mars will generate little green soldiers who like taking orders and being shot at, and ask for neither recompense nor recognition?

Speaking truth to power seems, when one looks at the juggernaut towering over us, to require some courage. But when one looks at the impossible tasks which the juggernaut is creating for itself, speaking truth offers the only conceivable prospect for a humane outcome to a monstrous gathering crisis.

Ken Coates

Will Iran Be Next?

Ken Coates

In his State of the Union speech in January 2002, President Bush set out a prospectus for the conduct of his war on terror. The destruction of the Twin Towers had exploded into universal shock, as, all around the world, people expressed their spontaneous sympathy with the victims who had perished in the World Trade Centre. There was genuine and widespread support for action against terrorism. But the United States Government chose to present its policy not as a police action, but as a 'war'. In the State of the Union address, President Bush began by saying:

> 'As we gather tonight, our nation is at war, our economy is in recession, and the civilised world faces unprecedented changes. Yet the state of our Union has never been stronger … The American flag flies again over our Embassy in Kabul. Terrorists who once occupied Afghanistan now occupy cells at Guantanamo Bay. And terrorist leaders who urged the followers to sacrifice their lives are running for their own.'

Of course, the war on terrorism was not a war within the conventional use of that term, as the American administration itself attested whenever it spoke, in equivocal terms, about 'military' action or when it established the prison camp of Guantanamo Bay, or devising an *ad hoc* justification for disregarding all the Geneva Conventions on the treatment of prisoners of war, and in the process denying due process to its captives. These detainees were to be interrogated, without any of the customary protections afforded to prisoners of war. From the moment of their original detention until the present day, in June 2003, few have been released, and none have had the protection of lawyers. Elaborate plans have been made to extend the facilities in Cuba, including the construction, in the Guantanamo Bay camp, of a 'death row' to handle the dispatch and disposal of those victims who are expected to be arbitrarily sentenced to death. President Bush's first priority in defining the

Ken Coates is editor of The Spokesman *and Chairman of the Bertrand Russell Peace Foundation.*

State of the Union was to take his war to persons accused of terrorism in other countries from Bosnia to the Philippines, and from Somalia to Pakistan.

But his second goal was

> 'to prevent regimes that sponsor terror from threatening America or our friends and allies with weapons of mass destruction. Some of these regimes have been pretty quiet since September the 11th. But we know their true nature. North Korea is a regime arming with missiles and weapons of mass destruction, while starving its citizens.
>
> Iran aggressively pursues these weapons and exports terror, while an unelected few repress the Iranian people's hope for freedom.
>
> Iraq continues to flaunt its hostility toward America and to support terror. The Iraqi regime has plotted to develop anthrax, and nerve gas, and nuclear weapons for over a decade. This is a regime that has already used poison gas to murder thousands of its own citizens – leaving the bodies of mothers huddled over their dead children. This is a regime that agreed to international inspections – then kicked out the inspectors. This is a regime that has something to hide from the civilized world.
>
> States like these, and their terrorist allies, constitute an axis of evil, arming to threaten the peace of the world. By seeking weapons of mass destruction, these regimes pose a grave and growing danger. They could provide these arms to terrorists, giving them the means to match their hatred. They could attack our allies or attempt to blackmail the United States. In any of these cases, the price of indifference would be catastrophic.'

Iraq has certainly been decisively dealt with. Although the whole country has been occupied, the alleged weapons of mass destruction have not yet been found, and the UN Inspectors who asked for more time to look for them have expressed the opinion that they may not be found. But the occupying armies have announced that they themselves now need more time to look.

This article is concerned to explore whether the prospectus of the axis of evil implies a succession of future wars. Today, as occupiers of Iraq, the USA adjoins both Iran and Syria. Given the public warnings, and the new opportunities, must we expect a military attack on Iran? The situation in North Korea is certainly fraught, but so are American relations with the neighbouring countries in the Far East. North Korea will have to be considered separately, and is no doubt already being considered separately by the planners in the Pentagon and the State Department. But Iran shares more than a frontier with Iraq, including not only what the Americans deem to be 'evil', but also many other attributes which they regard as unalloyed 'goods'. In particular, Iran is a major oil power, and control of its resources has already been a matter of contention with the United States over much of its recent history.

There are not a few signs that the American administration is readying itself for the next phase of its war. Ari Fleischer, the press secretary to the President, recently accused Iran of failing to take appropriate steps to detain Al Qaeda terrorists who were said to be hiding out within its territory. The CIA has let it be known that it does not believe this claim. Nonetheless, Fleischer insisted:

> 'The future of Iran will be determined by the Iranian people, and I think the Iranian people have a great yearning for Government that is representative of their concerns.'

Simultaneously, Western media began to present long interviews with the son of the deposed Shah, in which he protested his undying commitment to democracy and human rights. Of course, a long time has elapsed since the revolution which deposed the Shah, but perhaps it may be doubted whether this will prove long enough to have erased the memories of the Shah's phenomenal cruelties, and the bloodthirsty operation of his secret police, the Savak.

A long running allegation by the Americans against Iran has been the charge that their nuclear programme is designed to produce materials for nuclear weapons. Instead, the Iranians maintain it is designed to generate fuel for civilian reactors.

Not far behind the Americans stands the presence of Israel, a nuclear power which has already been responsible for the classic pre-emptive strike against an Iraqi nuclear power facility, and which might be tempted, if the circumstances were right, to repeat the experience against Iran. The American predilection for 'counter-proliferation', as opposed to non-proliferation, which gives them a self-nominated role as world policeman, does mean that the Iranian nuclear programme could figure as the trigger for a military collision.

At the end of May *The Times* reported that the Bush administration was deeply split about how to make the next move on Tehran. On May 26th, Defence Secretary Rumsfeld announced that Tehran 'should be on notice' that the United States will not permit Iran to try to remake neighbouring Iraq in its Islamic image.

Iranians have certainly been accused of backing the Supreme Council of the Islamic Revolution in Iraq, a prominent Shia group. Its leader was in exile for twenty-three years in Tehran. Ayatollah Muhammad Baqir Al-Hamin returned to Iraq after the American – British occupation to a profoundly emotional reception. The Ayatollah led a significant militia, which will no doubt remain an important influence in Iraq unless it is suppressed by the occupying armies. However, the presumption that the Shia communities are looking for a confrontation with the invading forces in Iraq is not at all true. Neither the Iraqi Shia nor their Iranian co-religionists will seek to provoke the Americans, and although they will exercise a serious influence in Iraq, all the evidence up to now has been that this will be orderly, and not disruptive. Present conflicts with the American occupiers are normally found in Sunni districts, not the Shia ones. Of course, if the Americans gratuitously seek to suppress the Shia communities, then all this could change: and another trigger point for threats against Iran could result. But it is not reasonable to assume that Iranians will be looking for such an outturn. The contrary is more likely to be true.

This has not prevented Donald Rumsfeld from reporting to the Council on Foreign Relations that the Iranians must not trespass into Iraq: 'such an effort' he said, 'would be aggressively put down'. However, Defence Secretary Rumsfeld was not averse to a reverse movement in which 'reformist Iranians might some day be able to topple the ruling Islamic leadership' in Iran. Indeed, the Project for the New American Century has long been advising Secretary of Defence Donald

Rumsfeld, on how to dispose of the ruling parties in Iran, Libya and Syria, after victory in Iraq. Of course, the Bush administration has more than one string to its bow, and is not dependent on overt military intervention. There have been many suggestions that it might be possible to foment a popular uprising to overthrow President Khatami. Funds have been established to foster 'democracy' in Iran, and to facilitate radio and television stations broadcasting into the country.

Reports in the British press, based on Rumsfeld's recent statement, gave the impression that Iran might become a target of American military action. This was denied in the *Financial Times* by Victoria Clarke, the Assistant Secretary of Defence for Public Affairs. Ms. Clarke cited Mr. Rumsfeld as saying about Iran:

> 'It's a country that has been unhelpful with respect to Iraq. It's being unhelpful today with respect to Iraq.'

US policy on Iran was, said Ms. Clarke,

> 'to recognise the "churning in that country" by the women and the young people and the pressure they are putting on a handful of clerics that control that regime. The Secretary for Defence stated further that US policy was not to engage with the top two layers of Iranian Government. Doing so could legitimate those leaders and discourage the Iranian people.'

No doubt the disagreements in the administration will have been greatly increased by the global reaction against the war on Iraq, and the complete failure of the Americans and the British to find justification for their claims about Iraq's programme of weapons of mass destruction.

This has given rise to a situation in which the *Financial Times* claims that:

> 'not even America's neoconservatives support an invasion of Iran. Pentagon analysts regard the idea as a dangerous fantasy. However, according to media reports, plans have been advanced for the armed destabilisation of the regime in Tehran by US-backed forces. And there are plenty of historical examples to demonstrate how insurgency in support of regime change can easily lead to full-scale war.'

Anatol Lieven, of the Carnegie Endowment for International Peace in Washington, points out in the same newspaper article (*FT* 9th June 2003), that Iran has a marked capacity to retaliate against any American attempts to destabilise the regime in Tehran, because of its residual influence over Iraqi Shias.

> 'The extent of Iranian influence among the Iraqi Shias is unclear, but Islamist groups among them have ambitions totally at odds with US aims, and a tremendous capacity for mass mobilisation.'

If the turbulence which confronts Britain and the US in Iraq today continues for a year, pegging both countries down in prolonged and increasingly difficult attempts to pacify the local population, Lieven believes that this can feed back into political turmoil within the occupying powers.

'That is all the more reason for America's allies to respond with great reserve to US demands for support. Above all, this is a time for the British government to use its influence in the US to avoid being sucked step by step into a repeat of the Iraq war.'

It would be unwise to assume that the British government is ready to accept such advice. A clear indication of the dangers comes from Tony Blair, as ever a faithful interpreter of his sponsors in the United States. On the 29th May, he was reported in the *Daily Mirror* as 'telling Iran not to develop nuclear weapons or support terrorists'. On the same day, the *Financial Times* reported that Blair warned

'Iran's hard-line clerics not to undermine the process of building a new Government in Iraq or the 'road map' to peace between Israel and the Palestinians'.

It was Blair's office which informed the press that Russia had agreed not to go ahead with plans to help the Iranians develop their nuclear programme. This report was subsequently denied by Alexander Rumyantsev who said:

'We will continue to fulfil our duties despite the fact that our position on this question is different to Washington's official view.'

The fact that the British Prime Minister has found it necessary to catch up all of these straws in the wind indicates that he is sensitive to American preoccupations with the number two component of the axis of evil. If the American juggernaut were to move again, Mr. Blair would surely seek a lift on it.

The engagement of the London satellite, no less than the hesitations of the hegemonic Washington power, still leave room for uncertainty about the outcome in Iran. But this should not be taken as evidence that peace movements need do nothing. On the contrary, it should be taken as an invitation to intensify their activities to prevent the bloody chapter which could very easily unwind in the coming months.

The CWU says

NO ONE WINS WARS *BUT* EVERYBODY PAYS

Communication Workers Union
150 The Broadway, Wimbledon, London, SW19 1RX
Tel: 020 8971 7200 Fax: 020 8971 7300
General Secretary: Billy Hayes
www.cwu.org

Iraq, the United States, and the end of the European coalition

Gabriel Kolko

We are experiencing the equivalent of a geopolitical earthquake.

The disintegration of the Soviet bloc permitted American unilateralism on a scale the modern world has never seen. But with its war against Iraq the United States for the first time openly massed its military power and then invaded another nation, justifying the war in the name of the elimination of weapons of mass destruction and 'regime change.' At the same time, it staked the very future of its existing alliances – NATO above all – but also the United Nations. NATO's demise is a major outcome of the war against Iraq. Washington wished to recast its European alliance, especially after its war against Serbia in the spring of 1999 revealed that the NATO principle of unanimity among its 19 members was a major inhibition on its freedom of action, but today its European coalition is disintegrating prematurely for reasons it both failed to anticipate and deplores. America's unilateralism and bellicosity has compelled some of the most important European nations to assert their independence well before they were ready or likely to do so.

Washington intended that NATO, from its very inception, serve as its instrument for maintaining its political hegemony over Western Europe, forestalling the emergence of a bloc that could play an independent role in world affairs. Charles de Gaulle, Winston Churchill, and many influential politicians envisioned such an alliance less as a means of confronting the Soviet army than as a way of containing a resurgent Germany as well as balancing American power.

Publicly, the reason for creating NATO in 1949 was the alleged Soviet military menace, but the United States always planned to employ strategic nuclear weapons to defeat the USSR – for which it did not need an alliance. But Washington believed that war with Russia was not imminent or even likely, a view that

Gabriel Kolko, the foremost historian of warfare, is the author of Another Century of War?

prevailed most of the time until the USSR finally disappeared. There was also the justification of preventing the Western Europeans from being obsessed with fear at reconstructing Germany's economy, and American military planners were concerned with internal subversion. But when the Soviet Union capsized over a decade ago, NATO's nominal rationale for existence died with it. But the principal reason for its creation – to forestall European autonomy – remains.

NATO provided a peacekeeping force in Bosnia to enforce the agreement that ended the internecine civil war in that part of Yugoslavia, but in 1999 it ceased being a purely defensive alliance and entered the war against the Serbs on behalf of the Albanians in Kosovo. The United States found the entire experience very frustrating. Targets had to be approved by all 19 members, any one of which could veto American proposals. The Pentagon's after-action report of October 1999 conceded that America needed the cooperation of NATO countries, but 'gaining consensus among 19 democratic nations is not easy and can only be achieved through discussion and compromise.' But Wesley Clark, the American who was NATO's supreme commander, regarded the whole experience as a nightmare – both in his relations with the Pentagon and NATO's members. '[W]orking within the NATO alliance,' American generals complained, 'unduly constrained US military forces from getting the job done quickly and effectively.'[1] A war expected to last a few days instead took 78 days. The Yugoslav war taught the Americans a grave lesson.

Long before September 11, 2001, Washington was determined to avoid the serious constraints that NATO could impose. However much their premises differ, Bush's closest advisers all believe in an apocalyptic world. Some, such as Vice-president Dick Cheney and Defense Secretary Donald H. Rumsfeld, are nationalists who believe America has overwhelming military power and should apply it. Others, such as Paul Wolfowitz, are neo-conservative ideologues, mainly Jewish academics and lawyers capable of articulating elegant Hobbesian justifications for the use of power – and wars; many are personally close to Israel's ruling Likud party. Their focus is mainly on altering fundamentally Middle Eastern politics to provide Israel a friendly geopolitical environment. Yet others, including the president, are born-again Christians who sincerely believe the United States has a divine mission to reorder the world. The White House has little patience with the increasingly impotent 'realists' and believers in traditional diplomacy in the State Department, much less those in the Central Intelligence Agency who believe that objective intelligence should influence foreign and military policies. Combined, this is an exceedingly dangerous intellectual cocktail to guide the most powerful nation on earth; its analytic basis for the application of power is highly romantic and dangerously irresponsible. Most of America's leaders are suspicious of foreigners, not just former enemies like Russia and China but also the major NATO allies, and they are quick – often nonchalant – to create adversarial situations with nations that criticise their blustering style in any way.

It is really quite misleading to concentrate exclusively on the systematic ideas and strategies of Bush's coterie, for the United States since at least 1949 has wanted military dominance, control over oil (principally at the expense of its British 'allies'), and the like – power in the largest geo-political sense. The errors built into this overweening ambition, from military 'credibility' to an ignorance of the political nuances and complexities of the nations the United States has sought to control, are many decades old. Like most persons who rise to the top in Washington, articulating great strategic designs comes easily to many of them. The real question is not systematic theories but the unintended consequences of grandiose, unrealistic ambitions and the loss of control over priorities: allies and proxies who collapse, as in the case of Thieu in Vietnam or the Shah in Iran, or become enemies – as with the Muslim fundamentalists in Afghanistan or Hussein in Iraq. For America always loses control of its priorities, especially insofar as the major regions of the world are concerned, and its grand plans have invariably fallen apart and frustrated.

This confusion and loss of priorities is best illustrated by the shifting importance of Asia in Washington's priorities. When the Bush Administration took power at the beginning of 2001 it was committed to a much more activist foreign policy in East Asia, and was especially resolved to confront China. Until September 11 China was the threat of choice to most of official Washington, a potential enemy big enough to justify the Pentagon's extravagant spending. The crash of an American spy plane with a Chinese fighter over Hainan island in April 2001 gave force to the imminent administration designation of China as the leading 'peer competitor' to the United States. September 11 changed everything, and wars in Afghanistan and Iraq have completely altered America's priorities. China is no longer of prime importance to it, and even North Korea's nuclear bombs remain a question it wavers on, and it is a challenge it is loath to confront soon because it lacks the military resources – it is spread far too thinly throughout the world. The war in Afghanistan destabilized the Musharraf regime in Pakistan, and South Asia with it – future relations between nuclear-armed India and Pakistan are more unpredictable than ever. As for the Western Hemisphere, which is essentially outside of the leading decision makers' vision, Washington has neglected and thereby alienated Mexico and Canada – its two neighbours and major trading partners – to an extent which was completely unintended.

One may look at America's resolve over the past two years and ultra-sophisticated military equipment as a sign of strength as well as imperialist pretension, but it is also an indication of endemic confusion and a policy that will unintentionally lead to the diffusion of its power – and create more weakness for it. This is the history of its improvised and often chaotic behaviour since 1945.

The people who lead the United States today do not think in these terms, because priorities and their systematic application imply constraints and a recognition of the limits of power, if only to exploit its formidable resources more rationally. For these men, the only question over the past several years was of timing and how the United States would escape NATO's clear military obligations while maintaining its political hegemony over its members. They still want to preserve NATO for the very reason it was established: to keep Europe from developing an independent political as well as military organisation. Some of its members want NATO to reach a partial accord with Russia, a relationship on which Washington often shifted, but Moscow remains highly suspicious of its plans to extend its membership to Russia's very borders. When the new administration came to power in January 2001, NATO's fundamental role was already being reconsidered. What it did add – at least as much out of ineptness as conscious policy – was a readiness to smash the alliance if necessary. For apart from their penchant for action, which in itself is scarcely unique, its spokesmen have a completely incompetent sense of public relations, creating shock and opposition among friends as well as enemies – and resistance to America's objectives well before it might otherwise occur. Although it would eventually have happened anyway, NATO's demise is a good example of this policy based on blunders whose unintended consequences then become decisive.

President Bush is strongly unilateralist, and he repudiated the Kyoto Protocol on global warming, opposes further restrictions on nuclear weapons tests or land mines, and is against a host of other existing and projected accords. He also greatly accelerated the development of an anti-ballistic missile system, which will give the United States a first-strike capacity and which China and Russia justifiably regard as destabilising – thereby threatening to renew the nuclear arms race. Downgrading the United Nations, needless to say, was axiomatic. The war in Afghanistan was fought without NATO but on the United States' terms by a 'floating' coalition 'of the willing,' a model for future conflicts 'that will,' according to Rumsfeld, 'evolve and change over time depending on the activity and circumstances of the country.' It accepted the small German, French, Italian, and other contingents that were offered only after it became clear that the war, and especially its aftermath, would take considerably longer than the Pentagon expected. But it did not consult them on military matters or crucial political questions.

Despite its military success, the Afghan war was a political failure for the United States. The country is today ruled by warlords, its economy is in a shambles, and even the Taliban is again attracting followers. The United States has never been able to translate its superior arms into political success, and that decisive failure is inherent in everything it attempts. Iraq is very likely to confirm this pattern; its regionalism and internecine ethnic strife will produce years of instability. Rational assessments of these repeated political failures would lead America to act far less frequently, and its vision consciously excludes alliances that will inhibit its actions.

The war with Iraq is only the first step in the United States' astonishingly ambitious project to recast the world. It has identified Iraq, Iran, and North Korea as members of an 'axis of evil.' Even today there is growing and formidable pressure on the Bush Administration to destroy Iran's nuclear facilities, thereby courting an even broader regional war. But as its 'Nuclear Posture Review' to Congress made clear in January 2002, Syria and Libya are also 'immediate' dangers, while China and even Russia 'remain a concern.' The Iraq war is the beginning of a cycle.²

On September 19, 2002 Bush proclaimed the United States' commitment to fighting 'pre-emptive' wars against 'rogue states' that have weapons of mass destruction or harbour 'terrorists.' His vision extends far beyond the constraints inherent in alliances, much less agreeing to conform to the decisions of the United Nations. This 'new' era in international relations, with momentous implications for war and world peace, in fact began long before then, but it was inevitable that the unilateralists now in charge of America's foreign policy would bring it to its logical conclusion.

Washington has decided that its allies must now accept its objectives and work solely on its terms, and it has no intention whatsoever of discussing the merits of its actions in NATO conferences. This applied, above all, to the war against Iraq – a war of choice.

The United States submitted the Iraq issue to the UN Security Council only because of a vain effort by Secretary of State Colin Powell to stem the unilateralism of the dominant entourage around President Bush, but the entire crisis revealed the impotence of traditionalists in the State Department. The Americans based their case for military action on the alleged existence of Iraqi weapons of mass destruction (WMD) as well as Hussein's purported links with Al Qaeda terrorists. But Israeli intelligence reported to the United States that Hussein had no ties whatsoever to Bin Laden. The CIA concurred, and many of its analysts complained publicly that the White House was forcing them to lie on this issue.

As for weapons of mass destruction, the United Nations inspectors did not find any and the CIA was convinced that by 1995 Hussein had few, if any, left. Much more important, he did not use them against the invading American army, which so far has not found any. The single most important US public justification for the Iraq war proved to be an utter falsehood. This catastrophic lie will haunt the United States for years to come, because although it proved in Iraq that it militarily could quickly defeat what was, at best, a second-rate army, it has no political credibility whatsoever. France saw the issue as primarily one of the rule of agreed international law in guiding international affairs of all nations, and regarded American behaviour as both arbitrary and unilateral. To this extent, the Iraq crisis was broader and impinges directly on NATO's future. The French and German refusal to support what was an obvious American obsession to eliminate a regime that it (and Israel) deplored was vindicated, although the Security Council could not constrain arbitrary and dangerous American action. But it embarked on war anyway. Its real goal was political – regime change – and it is the beginning of a cycle of interventions that may last years; its ultimate consequences are utterly unpredictable.

The crisis in NATO was both overdue and inevitable, the result of a decisive American reorientation, and the time and ostensible reason for it was far less important than the underlying reason it occurred: the United States' growing realisation after the early 1990s that while NATO was militarily a growing liability it still remained a political asset. The United Nations and Security Council were strained in ways that proved decisive, but the United States never assigned the UN the same crucial role as it did its alliance in Europe. The Iraq war was the final step in NATO's demise.

Today, NATO's original *raison d'être* for imposing American hegemony – which was to prevent the major European nations from pursuing independent foreign policies – is the core of the controversy that is now raging. Washington cannot sustain this grandiose objective because a reunited Germany is far too powerful to be treated as it was a half-century ago, and Germany has its own interests in the Middle East and Asia to protect. Germany and France's independence was reinforced by wholly inept American propaganda on the relationship of Iraq to Al Qaeda (from which the CIA and British MI6 openly distanced themselves), overwhelming antiwar public opinion in most nations, and a great deal of opposition within the United States establishment and many senior American officers to the war with Iraq. The furious American response to Germany, France, and Belgium's refusal, under article 4 of the NATO treaty, to protect Turkey from an Iraqi counter-attack because that would prejudge the Security Council's decision on war and peace was only a contrived reason for confronting fundamental issues that have simmered for years. The dispute was far more about symbolism than substance, and the point was made: some NATO members refused to allow the organisation to serve as a rubber stamp for American policy, whatever it may be. War in Iraq forced the issue to a head, compelling major NATO members and Russia to resist Washington's leadership. Whether such a split was inevitable is now moot – it happened.

Turkey's problem was simple: the United States pressured it, despite overwhelmingly antiwar Turkish public and political opinion, to allow American troops to invade Iraq from Turkey – in effect, to enter the war on its side. The United States wanted NATO to aid Turkey in order to strengthen the Ankara government's resolve to ignore overwhelmingly antiwar domestic opinion. The arms it was to receive were superfluous. But the Turks have always been far more concerned with Kurdish separatism in Iraq rekindling the civil war that Kurds have fought in Turkey for much of the past decade, and the conditions they demanded on these issues put Washington in a very difficult position from which it could not extricate itself. The United States naively took Turkey for granted, as it has for many decades, tying up its most modern armour division offshore its coast on the assumption it could also invade Iraq from the north. An important faction of the government deliberately protracted negotiations with the United States in the hope of preventing the war altogether.[3]

Turkey's best – and most obvious – defence was to stay out of the war, which the vast majority of Turks wanted. After incessant haggling, it ended up doing so, and its relations with the U.S. are now very strained, perhaps irreparably. Meanwhile, tens of thousands of Turkish troops are massed at the Iraq border and they will march if the Kurds keep Kirkuk, declare *de facto* independence, or in some way threaten Turkish interests. A crisis may not occur in the coming weeks, but it is a constant threat in the future. For the United States it is a nightmare which can easily become reality.

Geopolitically, the consummately ambitious American plan for restructuring the Middle East's politics, making it more congenial to itself as well as to Israel, is very likely to fail. Arab opinion – even among those once friendly to the United States – was overwhelmingly antiwar and passionately angry, a fact that will only increase terrorism's appeals and its dangers to Americans and their allies. The vast majority of Arabs believe that the outcome of the war on Iraq will be instability for the entire region.

There is no longer an Iraqi balance to Iranian predominance in the Gulf region, a fact that has untold geopolitical implications. Saudi Arabia at the end of April asked the United States to abandon its ultra-modern bases quickly, which it has agreed to do, and the Saudis have made a grudging move to make peace with the detested Iranian Shia regime. Washington supported Hussein in his war with Iran throughout the 1980s, providing him credits, intelligence, and vital military support, solely to contain Iran, and now Iraq is incapable of playing that role. Turkey is likely to intervene, one way or another, to control the Kurds in northern Iraq – what may occur there is wholly unpredictable and will be a vital question in the future. But while America will very likely keep a much larger military presence in the region for many years to come, using Iran as an excuse, it cannot oppose the Turks without shattering the illusion of its alliance with it – and NATO. War with Iraq has created a vast number of uncontrollable geopolitical dangers throughout the region.

Iran's role is of overwhelming importance to the United States – and to Israel. It is militarily far more formidable than Iraq and will have nuclear weapons in due course – the timing is much disputed. Iran's principal concern is Israel, its nuclear weapons and delivery systems, and Iran has neither the intention nor the technology to reach beyond it. The obvious solution is to create a nuclear-free zone enforced by international inspection, an option Israel is most unlikely to accept, and in late June Iran reiterated its commitment to a nuclear-weapons-free region. 'The war in Iraq is just the beginning,' former prime minister Shimon Peres said on Israeli television last February. Will the United States 'drain the swamp' in the region, as the neoconservatives advocate, even including Saudi Arabia among the regimes to be toppled?[4] Washington is divided on this specific issue but not on the question of its commitment to an aggressive foreign policy globally. What inhibits it most is Iraq's political chaos, which it may increasingly feel obligated to resolve before it confronts more wayward nations, and the immense costs of the American way of making war – costs its former allies are unwilling to share.

The End of Alliances

America still desires to regain the mastery over Europe it had during the peak of the Cold War but it is also determined not to be bound by European desires – or indeed by the overwhelming European public opposition to the war with Iraq.

Genuine dialogue or consultation with its NATO allies is out of the question. The Bush administration, even more than its predecessors, simply does not believe in it – nor will it accept NATO's formal veto structure; NATO's division on Turkey has nothing to do with it. Washington cannot have it both ways. Its commitment to aggressive unilateralism is the antithesis of an alliance system that involves real consultation. France and Germany are now far too powerful to be treated as obsequious dependents, and the meeting at the end of April between these two nations and Belgium – although still vague in its implications – is an important step in the direction of NATO's breakup and the creation of an autonomous bloc that Washington cannot control. These states also believe in sovereignty, as does every nation which is strong enough to exercise it, and they are now able to insist that the United States both listen to and take their views seriously. It was precisely this danger that the United States sought to forestall when it created NATO over 50 years ago.

The controversy over NATO's future has been exacerbated by Secretary of Defense Rumsfeld's attacks on 'Old Europe' and the disdain for Germany and France that he and his close adviser, Richard Perle, have repeated. But the underlying problems over the alliance's future have been smouldering for years. Together, the nations that opposed a pre-emptive American war in Iraq and the Middle East – an open-ended, destabilising adventure that is likely to last indefinitely – will influence Europe's future development and role in the world profoundly. Although they do not have armies comparable to the American, they have great and growing economies. If Russia cooperates with them, even only occasionally, they will be much more powerful, and President Putin's support for their position on the war makes that a real possibility.

Eastern European nations may say what Washington wishes on Iraq, but economically they are far more dependent on Germany and those allied with it. When the 15 nations in the European Union met last February 17 their statement on Iraq was far closer to the German-French position than the American, reflecting the anti-war nations' economic clout as well as the response of some pro-war political leaders to the massive anti-war demonstrations that have taken place in Italy, Spain, Britain and the rest of Europe. There is every likelihood that the United States will emerge from this crisis in NATO more belligerent, and more isolated and detested, than ever. NATO will then go the way of the South-East Asia Treaty Organisation (SEATO) and all of the other defunct American alliances.

The Bush administration does not believe it needs allies save on its own terms, and this erroneous presumption is changing the nature of global power and will lead to the United States being isolated. It is folly to guess the next American move, for the war in Afghanistan also destabilised Pakistan – a nuclear power – and North Korea is high on the President's list of evil states. Given its global ambitions and commitments, the United States may very well be drawn elsewhere, and soon. The men who lead it now are capable of anything. At the present time, the Pentagon is considering creating an American-trained and led international peacekeeping force wholly independent of the United Nations and NATO. It has already discussed the option with some European and Latin American nations. Such a force would be a major step in reinforcing Washington's unilateralism and eliminate UN and NATO restraints on it. One way or another, however, NATO's importance for the United States will decline.

The world has reached the most dangerous point in recent history, one full of threats of wars and instability unlike anything which prevailed when a Soviet-led bloc existed. The war against Iraq and those very likely to follow it are the logic of United States foreign and military policies, one that assumes it has a near monopoly of power, that emerged first after the collapse of Communism. The Bush administration has brought them to their inevitable culmination.

There should be no doubt that the Cold War geopolitical legacies are ending and a new configuration of nations is in the process of being created. It is a mistake to think that America's quick defeat of the demoralised, corrupt Iraqi regime reflects its new technological military prowess rather than Hussein's political weakness. Rumsfeld wishes to trumpet the strength of the Pentagon's arms but this conclusion is scarcely justified by the facts. Military triumph, in any case, can scarcely be equated with political success – and it is politics that counts most in the long run.

The reality is that the world is increasingly multipolar, economically and technologically, and that the United States' desire to maintain absolute military superiority over the world is a chimera. Russia remains a military superpower, China is becoming one, and the world should have confronted and stopped the proliferation of destructive weaponry 20 years ago. It can only be done, if it is still possible, by international accords and bodies – such as the United Nations – which the United States rejects as a constraint on its power. The United States has no alternative but to accept the world as it is, or prepare for doomsday.

Unfortunately, there is not the slightest indication America will acknowledge the limits of its aspirations. The crisis in NATO and the dissolution of its dominant role in Europe reflects this diffusion of all forms of power and the diminution of American hegemony, which remains far more an unattainable aspiration than a reality.

References
1. Secretary of Defense William S. Cohen and Gen. Henry H. Shelton, 'Joint Statement on the Kosovo After Action Review,' Senate Armed Services Committee, Oct. 14, 1999, p. 3.
2. *Capital Hill Blue*, Feb. 16, 2003; *Washington Post*, Feb. 7, 2003; *New York Times*, March 23, 2003.
3. *Washington Post*, Feb. 28, 2003.
4. *Haaretz*, March 20, 2003; *Milwaukee Journal Sentinel*, April 5, 2003.

Bakers, Food and Allied Workers Union

Welcomes

the

European Network for Peace & Human Rights

Best wishes for your work with activists in the Middle East and the United States

Joe Marino
General Secretary

Ronnie Draper
National President

Who rules the peace when the rulers break the rules?

Phyllis Bennis

Phyllis Bennis works at the Institute of Policy Studies, Washington DC. She is a Fellow of the Transnational Institute, for which she prepared the second part of this text.

I

The United States war on Iraq was waged without United Nations authority, and in violation of the UN Charter. It was a war of aggression. According to the Geneva Convention, as the occupying powers the United States and the United Kingdom are obligated to provide for the humanitarian needs of the Iraqi population, including food, medicine, water, shelter, etc. (Article 55 of the 4th Geneva Convention and Article 69 of the 1st Protocol). This obligation is unquestionable during the period of hostilities, as well as during any period of post-war United States occupation.

Because the war itself was illegal, any post-war US occupation is illegal too. That means the United States should not be allowed to claim any power to rule or determine economic, political or social arrangements in post-war Iraq. The United States and the United Kingdom are still, however, obligated to pay the cost of providing for the humanitarian needs of the occupied Iraqi people during the war and its aftermath. Only the United Nations has the legitimate authority to provide governance and to help rebuild a new Iraqi government and civil society once the incumbent Iraqi regime had been overthrown.

The United Nations itself pushed for a central role in emergency relief (particularly through the large international humanitarian agencies such as UNICEF and the World Food Program). In a difficult meeting with Kofi Annan, in the first days of the war, US National Security Adviser Condoleezza Rice essentially claimed the right to issue a diktat for the role of the United Nations in post-war Iraq. Annan indicated he did not believe the United Nations should be co-opted into providing the United States with *ex post facto* legitimation for its illegal war. According to Secretary of State Powell, however, two weeks into the war, 'what we have to work out is ... how the UN role will be used to provide some level of endorsement for our actions, the actions of the coalition in Iraq.'

The United States was determined that its military would rule Iraq when the war had ended. There was disagreement within the administration as to the balance of power between the overall Pentagon-chosen viceroy, and the State Department nominees to head the various shadow ministries, each of which was to be assigned several advisers from among the US-anointed Iraqi exiles. State Department officials indicated fear that Pentagon ideologues were trying to replace the State nominees with people like former CIA chief James Woolsey, a long-time campaigner for war against Iraq. But there was no recognition of the international obligations incumbent on what United Nations Secretary General Kofi Annan called the 'belligerent powers occupying Iraq.'

Testifying in Congress on March 26, Secretary of State Powell described the limits of what the potential United Nations role could be in decision-making regarding governance of post-war Iraq. A member of Congress asked him, 'it seems to me it's one thing for there to be a future UN resolution about a role for the UN, particularly humanitarian. But it would be another thing for the UN resolution to lay out some road map for post-war Iraq in such a way that it [the UN] would basically grab that decision-making and control from the coalition.... Can you give us some assurance that whatever UN resolutions are in the future will not do that?' Powell replied 'I don't even see a possibility of that right now. ... We would not support ...essentially handing everything over to the UN, for someone designated by the UN to suddenly become in charge of this whole operation.' Later in his testimony Powell said that, 'we didn't take on this huge burden with our coalition partners not to be able to have significant, dominating control over how it unfolds in the future.'

On the parallel question of paying the costs of emergency assistance and reconstruction, Powell was equally explicit. In the same March 26th testimony, he said, 'the UN has a role to play. If we want to get help from other nations, and we ask these nations to go get funds from their parliaments or their legislatures, it makes it a lot easier for them to get those funds and to contribute those funds to the reconstruction/redevelopment effort if it has an international standing, if I can put it that way, as opposed to "just give us money to give to the Americans." That will not work. And so there are a number of advantages to having a UN role in this effort.' But the United States remains very clear that while it expected international financial support to cover its own humanitarian obligations, it has no intention of sharing actual authority, power, or decision-making with anyone. BBC World quoted a high-ranking Bush administration official who was asked whether France should have a role. Referring to France's alleged 'anti-americanism,' the official said 'if they want to participate, they can pick up the garbage.'

Two weeks into the war senior Bush administration officials, responding to the 'overly optimistic' assumptions that governed their post-war planning, acknowledged that 'the American military will likely need to retain tight control over the country for longer than they anticipated.' (*New York Times*, 2 April 2003)

On the question of organising emergency humanitarian assistance, US military planners anticipated aid organisations would flood into Iraq as soon as the military fighting was over, providing sufficient food, medicine, shelter, water purification, etc., for the Iraqi population and operating under US military authority. The Pentagon wanted humanitarian workers to wear identification badges issued by the US Department of Defense. However, aid organisations themselves identified key problems: 1) there was insufficient food, medicine and water inside Iraq to provide for the population's needs once the immediate family-stored stocks have been used up; 2) during the war, the United States refused to grant permission for aid organisations to enter Iraq to assess needs and begin bringing in material – essentially the United States seized control of much of Iraq's border control and determined who may enter; 3) the continued existence of US-controlled economic sanctions meant that aid organisations could not get licenses to move significant amounts of goods into Iraq even to the limited degree they could safely do so; 4) aid organisations in general are not prepared to work under military control – such an arrangement compromises their mandatory neutrality, and places at risk all their counterparts elsewhere in the world who then become identified with the US military attack on Iraq.

The Pentagon created the Office of Reconstruction and Humanitarian Assistance, initially run by former General Jay Garner, who was previously based in Kuwait and answered to General Tommy Franks, CentCom chief and head of the US military attack. Garner remained, despite his new Iraq post, the President of SY Technology, which provides technical support for missile systems used in the Iraq war. The appointment of Garner reflected several layers of problems: 1) he represented the intersection of military brass and weapons manufacturers that is inherently suspect; 2) he has made provocative statements regarding the capability of weapons (including a widely disputed claim about the Patriot missile) and about Israel ('Israel has exercised remarkable restraint in the face of lethal violence orchestrated by the leadership of a Palestinian authority') and was certain to provoke extreme reactions in the Arab world; 3) he was known to have 'frosty' and 'strained' relations with the United Nations; 4) appointing any American to act as pro-consul in Iraq following an illegal war represents further defiance of the UN Charter and the authority of the United Nations.

The US planned for the Agency for International Development (AID) staff to work under Pentagon control in co-ordinating aid efforts after the war, essentially relegating even Washington's own premier aid agency to becoming an arm of the military.

Philip E. Carroll, the former chief executive officer of the giant Shell Oil Company was the likely appointee of the Bush administration to 'oversee' post-war Iraqi oil production. He recently retired as chairman and chief executive officer of Fluor Corporation, a construction company singled out as one of the five US firms offered massive contracts by the Pentagon for rebuilding Iraq.

According to the *New York Times*, Carroll is known for not micro-managing people, something the *Times* says would serve him well 'If the administration decides to let the Iraqis control their oil.'

What do we call for?

The United Nations must be in charge of emergency and post-war reconstruction efforts, not the United States.

The United States and the United Kingdom as belligerent occupying powers are liable under the Geneva Conventions for costs of emergency and post-war reconstruction efforts.

During hostilities the belligerent powers are obligated to provide for the needs of the civilian population. Humanitarian organisations must be given free access to the country and allowed to do their work, to bring in people and supplies unhindered by military restrictions or the limitations imposed by sanctions, and must be allowed to make their own decisions regarding when it is safe to enter the country. They must be independent of, not under the control of, the US military.

No US officials with ties to the Pentagon or to arms manufacturers whose weapons are currently deployed against Iraqis should be allowed to participate in any post-war humanitarian position.

Going Global: Building a Movement Against Empire

II

As the Bush administration strengthens its military victory and consolidates its occupation of Iraq, it continues its trajectory towards international expansion of power and global reach. The arrogance of its triumphalism, ignoring civilian carnage and dismissing the destruction of the ancient cities because, in Rumsfeld's words, 'free people have the right to do bad things and commit crimes,' reflects the hubris of ancient empires. Shakespeare's 'insolence of office' could well describe the contempt with which the Pentagon warriors look down on the peoples of the world.

The US war in Iraq is certainly not the first time the United States has unilaterally, illegally, and without justification attacked another country. But in the past – whether Grenada, Panama, the first Gulf War, even Kosovo – Washington generally attempted to validate its wars through some kind of claim (however spurious) of international legality. In giving life to Bush's doctrine of pre-emptive war, the assault on Iraq represents the first time a US president has claimed – even boasted – that he had the right to launch such a unilateral attack against a country that had not attacked the US and did not pose any imminent threat, and that international authority was unnecessary.

Claiming the right of pre-emptive war would not, by itself, be proof of empire. Even launching a war more accurately defined as an aggressive preventive war (since a pre-emptive attack implies an imminent threat) does not by itself represent such proof. But the eagerness of Washington's powerful to launch this war, without United Nations authorisation and with such reckless disregard for the consequences, with the expressed aim of toppling the government of an independent country, albeit one mortally wounded from war and twelve years of murderous sanctions, may represent just such proof.

Certainly one can argue, as Paul Schroeder does, that there is a critical distinction between hegemony and empire. (The History News Network, Center for History and the New Media, George Mason University, February 3, 2003.) 'Hegemony,' he writes, 'means clear, acknowledged leadership and dominant influence by one unit within a community of units not under a single authority. A hegemon is first among equals; an imperial power rules over subordinates. A hegemonic power is the one without whom no final decision can be reached within a given system; its responsibility is essentially managerial, to see that a decision is reached. An imperial power rules the system, imposes its decision when it wishes.'

Schroeder concludes that the United States 'is not an empire – not yet.' Writing some weeks before Washington's invasion of Iraq, he describes the United States as 'at this moment a wannabe empire, poised on the brink. The Bush Doctrine proclaims unquestionably imperialist ambitions and goals, and its armed forces are poised for war for empire – formal empire in Iraq through conquest, occupation, and indefinite political control, and informal empire over the whole Middle East through exclusive paramountcy.'

The rapid overthrow of the Iraqi regime, with its attendant moments of exhilaration and long hours of horror for tens of thousands of Iraqi civilians, has pushed Bush administration officials over that brink. Their smug 'other Middle Eastern governments better learn their lesson' attitude indicates an even fortified sense of self-righteousness and the justice of their cause. If Washington has not yet consolidated its global empire, the drive towards it is now undeniable.

Ultimately though, what is key is less the debate over whether the United States today is an aggressive hegemon or an imperial centre bound for global domination, than understanding the political significance and consequence of this historical moment. US tanks control the Euphrates valley and US troops occupy the sites of the earliest recorded history of humanity. But US policymakers willing to look out beyond their own euphoria will see not only a devastated and dishonoured Iraq facing at best an uncertain and difficult future; not only an Iraqi population whose largest components are calling equally for 'No to Saddam Hussein' and 'No to the United States' in their street protests; but as well a humiliated and enraged Arab world; a shattered system of alliances; and a constellation of international opposition growing that includes Washington's closest allies and an emerging global people's movement saying 'no' to Washington's war, and 'no' to Washington's empire.

If war in Iraq were the only clear imperial thrust of the Bush administration, it would be tempting to reduce it to the resource-grabbing of an oil industry administration, the actions of an irresponsible hegemony soon to be taken to task by the rest of the global community of units. Opposition to the war could indeed be reduced to the demand of 'no blood for oil.' But when taken in the context of even longer-standing, and more visionary efforts to reshape regional and global power relations, the Iraq war emerges far more as exemplar of a broad and entrenched pattern, than as an isolated proof of US intent.

That is particularly significant in light of the combination of military, political, and economic factors whose collective expansion undergirds the relentless drive for power and empire. Militarily, the creation of a network of permanent bases throughout the Middle East and Central Asia, the Pentagon's techno-lethal 'revolution in military affairs,' the scaffolding of Israel's rise as an unchallengeable regional military power, and most especially the public commitment to a new generation of nuclear weapons designed for actual battlefield use, have contributed to a military capacity so enormous that no combination of other countries could even hope to approach, let alone match or surpass it.

Elsewhere in the world, US military involvement is on the rise in Latin America, particularly in Colombia, despite some emerging gains for popular forces elsewhere on the continent. In Africa, US military aid to oil-producing countries (such as Nigeria) is on the rise. In Asia, the United States is rebuilding its military connections with the Philippines, and discussions are continuing with Japan regarding expansion of Tokyo's military capacity and especially eliminating the now-contentious Article VI of Japan's constitution that prohibits the use of military force other than in self-defence. Washington is goading an unstable North Korea into consistently higher levels of nuclear brinkmanship, almost daring China to rise to the bait.

All over the world, the United States is reclaiming access to bases lost earlier to the vagaries of post-Cold War and post-neo-colonial politics – in places such as Yemen, Somalia, Ethiopia, the Philippines. The Bush administration's September 2002 national security statement refers directly to maintaining the enormous military chasm between the military capacity of the United States and the rest of the world, calling for the use of military force to insure that no nation or group of nations ever imagines even matching, let alone surpassing, US prowess.

The cavalier dismissal of concerns regarding increasing regional instability as a likely result of war in Iraq reflects a rash acceptance of the view that every political challenge has a military answer. And earlier, abandoning the Comprehensive Test Ban Treaty and essentially consigning the Non-Proliferation Treaty to the dustbin of history were part of the assertion of military unilateralism as a point of legitimate principle.

Economically, both internationally and domestically, it is clear that consolidation of economic power in fewer and fewer hands remains a key strategic approach of the administration. The Bush team continues its enthusiasm for domestic tax breaks for the rich and lack of concern with the dire domestic economic consequences of their $100-200 billion war in Iraq. The post-war contract-grab and war profiteering for administration-linked companies in Iraq reflects the broader privatisation focus of Bush foreign policy.

Abroad, the United States continues its agenda of advancing corporate trade and investment rights, as it attempts to craft a new round of global trade talks in the World Trade Organisation. Over the past six months Washington has blatantly tried to use economic aid and trade agreements as carrots and sticks to bribe, threaten and purchase coalition partners for the war in Iraq. (Although it was in this area, particularly the refusal of the 'Uncommitted Six' in the UN Security Council to sign on to Bush's 'coalition of the willing,' that Washington's failure was most visible.) And, the continuing moves to tighten US control over strategic oil and gas reserves in the Middle East and Central Asia are aimed at providing more economic clout to Washington *vis-à-vis* its economic competitors and allies.

Politically and diplomatically, Washington's effort to undermine and render 'irrelevant' the United Nations in the run-up to the Iraq war, clearly demonstrated the view of key Bush administration ideologues that UN authorisation was not only unnecessary but actually damaging to the holy grail of legitimising the unilateral assertion of US power. Coming on the heels of earlier rejections of treaty obligations and/or negotiations (Kyoto, the Anti-Ballistic Missile Treaty, the International Criminal Court, etc.) the Bush administration's grudging and dismissive use of the United Nations went far beyond the Clinton administration's cynically instrumentalist view of the UN as what Madeleine Albright famously called 'a tool of American foreign policy.' The Bush White House dismissed any notion of accountability to international law or the UN Charter, operating instead on a litany of assertions that UN resolutions meant whatever President Bush said they mean, and that anyway we don't need any UN resolutions, we have the god-given right to go to war when and where and against whom and for as long as we like. As George Monbiot recently wrote,

> 'the US, in other words, seems to be ripping up the global rulebook. As it does so, those of us who have campaigned against the grotesque injustices of the existing world order will quickly discover that a world with no institutions is even nastier than a world run by the wrong ones. Multilateralism, however inequitable it may be, requires certain concessions to other nations. Unilateralism means piracy: the armed robbery of the poor by the rich. The difference between today's world order and the one for which the US may be preparing is the difference between mediated and unmediated force.' (Guardian – 25/02/2003)

Moving Against Empire: The Second Super-Power?

There is no country or group of countries capable of launching a military challenge to Washington's power drive. But for perhaps the first time since the end of the Cold War, there is a serious competitor challenging the US empire for influence and authority – global public opinion, including a mobilised international civil society joined by key governments as well as the United Nations itself. Not only the Non-Aligned stalwarts of South Africa, Cuba, Malaysia, although they are vital to this challenge. Not only the key US allies such as France, Germany, or Russia eager to remain on good terms with Washington but clear about the danger of an unrestrained rogue empire. Not only the UN secretariat, facing extraordinary pressure to cave in to Washington's will yet aware that the global organisation's real survival depends on its willingness and ability to stand defiant of that pressure in defence of the UN Charter.

But all of those forces together make up the astonishing movement towards a new internationalism that today forms the global challenge to the empire. And the United Nations, while not the only sector, is at its centre.

We are living through an extraordinary historical moment. The combination of events in mid-February 2003 – the unprecedented Security Council response to de Villepin's call to defend the United Nations as an instrument of peace and not a tool for war and the resulting refusal of the Council and its members to accede to US demands, and the outpouring of millions across the globe on February 15 when 'The World Says No to War,' *and* the amazing reaction to those demonstrations by the United States, United Kingdom and other governments – provided even clearer evidence that we are at a critical historical juncture. The *New York Times* analysis defined this as a moment proving that once again there are two superpowers in the world '– the United States, and global public opinion.'

Although that global movement against war in Iraq failed to stop the US onslaught, it is in the process of transformation into a movement against the emerging US empire. Many of the speakers at many of the simultaneous February 15th rallies around the world hit the same point – this war, and this anti-war movement, are no longer just about Iraq. This is about mobilising the world against the United States. To the shock of ideologically-driven American analysts, European and other governments recognised that the need to constrain the United States is as urgent – or more so – as the need to restrain Baghdad – and that effort was reflected in the UN debate. Writing in the the *New York Times* magazine, James Traub quoted an unnamed UN official saying that the Security Council members ended up feeling that they had to stand up to American unilateralism.

It was in this context that the conscious struggle – and again with the United Nations as the primary venue – emerged among Europeans. Old Europe recognised the danger of ignoring the rise of US power, and sought to go public with the long-denied goal of building Europe as an explicit counterweight to the United States. Public opinion in France, Germany and elsewhere made it possible – indeed virtually mandatory – for those governments to stand defiant of the United States in the Security Council, making what likely began as a tactical disagreement with Washington into a point of principle. The new European governments, still caught up in the illusion of taking advantage of the European Union's generous cash benefits while keeping their strategic eggs solidly in Washington's basket, faced 65-80% public opposition to their support for Bush's war. Differences over the nature of an expanded Europe, then, emerged as a crucial sub-text within United Nations debates.

The events of February 15 transformed a widespread anti-war sentiment into a powerful global movement, one that was mobilised around the world on the same slogan – 'The World Says No to War'. It wasn't simply a matter of simultaneous demonstrations – there was the qualitatively greater power that comes from a shared framework (even if spontaneous and rudimentary rather than conscious and comprehensive). It was that connection and co-ordination that set in motion Washington's and other international ruling class recognition of the importance of our movement, at a moment when élite opposition had been largely squelched within US domestic politics.

For the moment the main focus must remain on Iraq – because even the millions of people in the streets around the world couldn't reverse Bush's military course, and with Iraq laid to ruin the work of our anti-war movement isn't done yet. But what's clear is that a quickly increasing number of people within that movement understand it as part of a much bigger, global mobilisation against a much bigger threat even than devastating war in Iraq.

The arguments shaping that movement are only now being woven into a coherent whole. They start with condemning the civilian lives lost and massive destruction in Iraq, warning of regional instability throughout the Middle East and the possibility of increased terrorism world-wide as a result of the war, exposing the increased economic costs of the war and their impact on the poorest strata in the United States and elsewhere, including the virtual abandonment of already-insufficient economic aid to Africa. Even before the war began the movement was developing clarity on issues of US hypocrisy regarding its own role in Iraq's weapons of mass destruction programmes, double standards regarding UN resolutions, and the massive Iraq resource-grab inherent in the hand-out of multi-billion dollar contracts to Bush administration corporate minions and cronies.

As the movement's parameters expand, the broader articulation frames the Bush administration's global trajectory and explains the connections within it. Those include the links between Iraq and Israel-Palestine; between oil, Central Asia, and the unfinished Afghanistan war; between pre-emptive war doctrine and aggressive preventive wars; between North Korean nukes and Israel's nuclear arsenal; Syria, Iran and weapons of mass destruction; corporate domination and military spending; US power projection and local budgets; building a new internationalist movement and the role of the United Nations.

The issue of the UN role in the Iraq crisis alone is widely misunderstood and confusing for many people. The question of whether the United Nations, dominated by the United States, is primarily a villain or a victim in situations like that surrounding the Iraq war, remains unresolved among many parts of the activist movement. Should the global organisation be defended from US attack, or targeted as imperialism with a global face? Recognition of the United Nations' potential as a centre of opposition to US hegemonic moves, while understanding the constraints imposed on the organisation and the need for civil society to defend it from the ravages of US power, is not widespread. The organisations created to defend the United Nations have served largely as cheerleaders, afraid or unable to articulate the political context of the current anti-UN crusade. And many within the broader peace movement remained confused, seeing the United Nations' silences in the face of the US war build-up as evidence of collaboration with the war. In autumn 2002/winter 2003, the refusal of the six Non-Aligned Security Council members to cave in to Washington's extraordinary pressure to endorse the US war was amazing. But it remains insufficiently appreciated in many quarters.

US pressure on the United Nations continues. Along with other coercion, the threatening letters sent to most UN member states in February 2003 demanding that they refuse to consider a General Assembly debate on Iraq, seem to have worked. An international team of activists continues its campaign to urge the General Assembly to take up the issue, challenging Security Council primacy, pushing for a UN condemnation of the war and empowered UN leadership in the political and humanitarian reconstruction of Iraq.

In examining the composition of the emerging movement against empire, it is notable that in key countries where governments stood defiant of the US war – including France, Germany, Brazil, the Philippines and many other countries – the peace movements are made up of largely the same forces as the anti-corporate globalisation or global justice movements. Their demands for a more equitable, just and sustainable global order, even while pressing the need for peace, provide a key framework for global mobilisation. And the nuanced political framework required to recognise the role Paris or Berlin play as part of the global front against US empire, while rigorously challenging their corporate-driven economic trajectory as well as other domestic and foreign policies, is beginning to take shape.

We are engaged now in building a global movement for peace and justice in a new kind of world – and we need a new global strategy. It will take some time for a unifying agenda for the global peace and justice movement to emerge. One feature will have to include universal disarmament, focusing first on the largest nuclear/military powers, including the United States. Another will be the focus on economic justice as a linchpin of social mobilisation. Other issues should include the primacy of internationalism and the centrality of the United Nations in all our work. That means claiming the United Nations as our own, as part of the global mobilisation for peace, and working to empower the United Nations as the legitimate replacement for the United States empire we seek to disempower. Even now, in Iraq, we must emphasise the need for the United Nations, not the Pentagon, to take charge of not only the humanitarian crisis but the move to create a new government.

It is at the centre of this movement against empire that the Transnational Institute is situated today. Our movement is broader and more complex than ever, being made up both of states and governments, and regional and international organisations including the United Nations, *and* the growing popular anti-war/global justice movements. That breadth provides both the promise of new power and influence, as well as extraordinary complexity and the need for strategic creativity involving careful combinations of inside-outside approaches to governments and multilateral organisations. The Transnational Institute, with ties to key activists and organisations central to the broad people's movements, as well as links to key governments and inter-governmental organisations, is one of the few international centres positioned to play a vital role (in the original, not the Bush-Blair meaning) in building the global movement against empire in this new period.

Responding to the more-or-less spontaneous emergence of this global movement means helping provide a space for strategic planning among key actors in the key countries, and helping to shape a political/intellectual framework on which a world-wide peace and justice movement can transform itself into a politically conscious movement challenging empire while building a new internationalism.

Public and
Commercial
Services Union

PCS, the largest civil service union stands for:

- **protecting public services**
  - **fair pay and pensions**
    - **world peace and social justice**
      - **an end to poverty and exploitation**

Janice Godrich
President

Mark Serwotka
General Secretary

The War on Freedom and Democracy

Tony Bunyan

Tony Bunyan, editor of Statewatch, presented this analysis of the effects of the 'war on terrorism' on civil liberties and the democratic culture of the European Union at the Conference of the European Network for Peace and Human Rights in Brussels.

The 'war on terrorism' has turned into an ongoing 'war on freedom and democracy' which is now setting new norms – where accountability, scrutiny and human rights protections are luxuries to be curtailed or discarded in defence of 'democracy'.

Introduction

Has the world changed after 11 September 2001? The answer is surely yes, but not in the way that Bush (and his allies) mean. We have seen a 'sea change' of great magnitude as we enter a second era of Western imperialism, or rather a new version of US imperialism – unlike the Cold War period the United States is no longer dependent on 'allies' or 'coalitions' (though these are useful to legitimate their actions).

But there is another difference between the Cold War era and the new one.

We now have a political system at the national and European Union levels which not only lacks content and accountability, but more importantly lacks a belief in the liberal democratic system itself. Government ministers and officials state that the European Union is 'democratic' (as is every EU Member State) and this together with 'freedom' is what the 'war on terrorism' is all about. But their actions speak a different language and have done for some time.

It can be argued that the high point in the development of liberal democracy was during the Cold War.[1] During this period liberal democracy had to have some substance, some tangible reality in opposition to Soviet-style communism. With the fall of the Berlin Wall in 1989 it was not just the USSR that disappeared but with it, too, the content of liberal democracy's political culture.

The end of the Cold War was a 'victory' for capitalism over the command economy but it was a triumph for economics rather than politics. There was no guarantee that liberal democracy as we had known it would survive. At a seminar on the third world and 'liberal democracy' at Wilton Park (a United Kingdom government sponsored think tank) in 1996, the recorded conclusion stated:

> Democracy must not be confused with capitalism. The former is a political system while the latter is an economic system. Although many capitalist countries are democracies, capitalism can exist without democracy[2]

Principles gave way to pragmatism, the retention of power became the primary aim of western political parties.

Of course European Union ministers and officials will simply argue: what is the problem? All the member states of the European Union are democracies and all are signed up to the European Convention on Human Rights (ECHR) – our freedoms and rights are therefore safe.

A democracy, or rather a liberal democratic political culture, is not simply about elections every four or five years and a worthy court in Strasbourg which is able to deal with some of the worst excesses. Rather a healthy democratic political culture is one that is diverse, informed, discursive, pluralistic, multicultural, and tolerant of peoples and their ideas.

It is also a culture that has a sense of history which informs the present and guides the future.

It is a culture that is not limited by parliamentarianism but rather one that encourages all elements in civil society.[3]

Nor is it a culture where most research is funded by and for the state. It is rather a culture where critical views are encouraged not marginalised.

The state of the 'European' democratic culture is even weaker than that at the national level. There is: i) a lack of informed scrutiny by parliaments and civil society of new measures introduced; ii) there are no mechanisms in place to monitor the practices (implementation) that flow from new measures; iii) there is no real freedom of information; iv) no real involvement of independent civil society (by which I mean groups not funded by the institutions); and finally, v) a quiescent, compliant media.

The most critical area of European Union activity, the one that most affects peoples' liberties, is the field of European Union justice and home affairs, the so-called 'area of freedom, security and justice'. Its origins lie in the 'Trevi' period. The Trevi *acquis*, 1976-1993, was incorporated into the Maastricht *acquis*,[4] 1993-1999. The Trevi and Maastricht *acquis*, together with the Schengen *acquis* (1985-1999), were bequeathed to the Amsterdam period *acquis*.[5]

These *acquis* are comprised of over 700 measures, some binding (for example, Conventions and Joint Actions) some intergovernmental (for example, Recommendations, Conclusions). The full *acquis*, as determined by the European Union, has to be adopted and implemented by applicant countries *in toto* – they are not allowed to make any changes whatsoever.[6]

What characterises this whole swathe of measures, and resulting practices, is that there was virtually no meaningful parliamentary scrutiny, let alone the chance for civil society to have any say or influence. Even now, under the Amsterdam Treaty, national parliamentary scrutiny reserves (where they exist) are routinely noted then ignored by the governments. The European Parliament is 'consulted' on Title IV (Treaty Establishing the European Community) immigration and asylum issues and on Title VI (Treaty on European Union) police and legal cooperation – but its views too are routinely ignored.

From well before 11 September there was evidence in the European Union that democratic standards were slipping on issues like civil liberties, data protection, scrutiny and accountability, legal protections and the rights of refugees and asylum-seekers fleeing from poverty and oppression.

We have, in effect, a European Union 'democracy' built on sand. A democracy which has little meaningful legitimacy. Thus, there was in place a democratic culture which was very poorly placed to resist the kind of attacks on liberties and rights we are now witnessing. Post 11 September there has been at the European Union level (as well as the national level) an avalanche of:
– new measures
– new practices
– new databases
– new *ad hoc* unaccountable groups
most of which have little to do with countering terrorism but rather concern:
– crime in general;
– the targeting of refugees, asylum-seekers, the resident migrant population, and protests and protestors;
– the creation of a 'United States-European Union axis' for co-operation on border controls, immigration, extradition and other legal co-operation.

Let us look at a few examples.

The European Union definition of terrorism

Two new measures were rushed through the European Union (Council and European Parliament) and national parliamentary scrutiny before Christmas 2001.[7] These were the Framework Decision on combating terrorism and the Framework Decision on a European arrest warrant.

The Framework Decision on combating terrorism was drafted by the European Commission and its publication was immediately criticised because it overtly referred to its potential use against 'urban violence' in the Explanatory Memorandum, and the Commission's website said measures were intended to counter 'radicals committing violence'. At the time, in late September, it was very hard to make *any criticism,* but we and others did. There was literally a six week period when no-one in Brussels, including the European Parliament, would listen. Then the reaction from many groups in civil society began to produce some effect. However, we also knew that events in Gothenburg and Genoa (where protestors had been shot by police and one killed) were still fresh in the minds of Ministers and officials. Whatever the eventual wording, we knew that the majority of European Union governments viewed protests at least as 'quasi-terrorist'.

In the end a Statement (which has no legal status or effect) was attached to the

Framework Decision seeking to distinguish between 'terrorists' and the right to demonstrate in democracies. But the wording of the measure remained ambiguous. Article 1 defined 'Terrorist offences' and says that each European Union Member State must ensure that the term covers:

> the following list of intentional acts which, given their nature and context, may seriously damage a country or an international organisation, as defined as offences under national law, where committed with the aim of:
> (i) seriously intimidating a population, or
> (ii) unduly compelling a Government or international organisation to perform or abstain from performing any act, or
> (iii) seriously destabilising or destroying the fundamental political, constitutional, economic or social structures of a country or an international organisation

It then lists a number of offences, many of which are obvious (for example, murder). However, under Article 1.iii.e. these offences include:

> 'causing extensive destruction of a Government building or public facility, a transport system, an infrastructure facility, including an information system, a fixed platform located on a continental shelf, a public place or private property likely to endanger human life or result in major economic loss'

There are millions and millions of people who, quite rightly, want governments and/or international organisations (for example, NATO, the World Trade Organisaton, and so on) to 'perform or abstain' from many acts. If this 'aim' is furthered by demonstrations/protests which result – for whatever reason – in or are likely to result in, for example, extensive damage to private property resulting in a major economic loss then these people become 'terrorists' through the effect of their actions.

Perhaps as telling as the formal decision was the refusal of the majority of European Union governments to explicitly remove any potential use of the Decision against those exercising their democratic rights. Equally contradictory was a refusal (though mentioned in the 'Statement') to exclude liberation struggles fighting against repressive and authoritarian regimes (many of which are supported by Western governments). On the other hand, 'actions by the armed forces of a State in the exercise of their official duties are not governed by this Framework Decision'.

This was complemented by further decisions taken by 'written procedure' (that is, proposals are circulated and agreed if no Member State objects) on 27 December 2001 (the day after Boxing Day). The measures, in part, implemented the United Nations Security Council resolution 1373 and extended the definition of terrorism to include 'active or passive' support for terrorist organisations and introduced the principle that security services should vet all asylum applications.

European arrest warrant

Another 'emergency' measure that went through all the legislative stages in weeks was the Framework Decision on the European arrest warrant. This does away with almost all of the checks and balances of the existing extradition procedure. For a list of 32 offences there will now be no legal test in the requested state. The requesting state simply has to say that a person is wanted for one of the listed offences and this person can be arrested – their homes searched and property seized – and deported to stand trial. There is no habeas corpus, no appeal, and few rights for the suspect.[8]

Exchanging 'information' on terrorists or protestors?

The Framework Decision on combating terrorism is binding and has to be incorporated into national law across the European Union (and the applicant countries). However, its contradictory ideology contaminates other measures, too. For example, the Recommendation proposed by the Spanish Presidency, adopted without debate by Justice and Home Affairs Ministers on 13 June 2002, for the 'introduction of a standard form for exchanging information on terrorists'. The Recommendation says the information to be exchanged should concern 'individuals with a criminal record in connection with terrorism as defined in the Framework Decision on combating terrorism'. The meaning of a 'criminal record' can vary from state to state and could simply cover, for example, people arrested for sitting down non-violently in the road.

The suspicion that the definition of 'terrorism' is being widened by the measure is reinforced by Recommendation 1 which says the purpose is to prevent:

> 'activities carried out by terrorist organisations to achieve their criminal aims at large international events'

and Recommendation 4 which speaks of:

> 'organised groups run by terrorist organisations for the purpose of achieving their own destabilisation and propaganda aims'

The rationale is plainly ludicrous. There have been no terrorist attacks on European Union Summits or international meetings held in the European Union. No members of Al Qaeda or any other terrorist group have ever been seen handing out leaflets at such meetings to 'propagandise' their aims. The absurdity is well illustrated by the reply of a United Kingdom Home Office Minister to the House of Lords Select Committee on the European Union. The Minister wrote:

> 'this initiative is essentially about ensuring that those hosting large international events within the EU are informed that known terrorists with a police record intend travelling to the event in question with the intent of furthering their aims'

Does this mean that there are dozens, if not hundreds, of *known* terrorists wandering around the European Union who have not been arrested, charged, convicted and imprisoned? Clearly not. The intent was not to deal with suspected terrorists, who are tracked by the internal security agencies and special anti-terrorist squads. Rather it is to counter protests and protestors. As set out in the first draft of the measure (but amended later), it is to deal with:

> incidents caused by violent radical groups with terrorist links... and where appropriate, prosecuting violent urban youthful radicalism increasingly used by terrorist organisations to achieve their criminal aims, at summits and other events arranged by various Community and international organisations

The Spanish Presidency proposal started out as a Framework Decision but ended as an intergovernmental 'Recommendation' – which did not have to be submitted for scrutiny to national or European parliaments. The exchange of information, through the secure European Union internal security agencies BDL (*Bureau de Liaison*) e-mail network, is likely to be extensively used by Spain, Portugal, Italy, France and Germany to target protest groups.

That such a measure could pass through the European Union, without proper parliamentary scrutiny, is worrying in itself. Its adoption confirms fears that the definition of terrorism has been broadened. Moreover, it adds to the measures already in place to counter protests: i) the Justice and Home Affairs Conclusions of 13 July 2001 putting in place surveillance of protest groups; ii) the plan to create a new database on the Schengen Information System (SIS) on protestors; iii) the plan agreed to bring together para-military police units (for example, carabineri, CRS, Tactical Support Groups in the UK) for European Union Summits and international meetings.

The surveillance of telecommunications

The paucity of the political culture has left the door open to other powerful influences, especially for state officials and agencies and international fora.

A classic case is the long-standing demand of the European Union's law enforcement agencies (police, customs, immigration and internal security) for the retention of telecommunications data and their access to it. The saga began in the summer of 1993 when the FBI called a meeting at its headquarters in Quantico and invited a number of European Union countries. The International Law Enforcement Seminar (ILETS) was set up to continue the discussion and this in turn fed into a G8 sub-group discussion on the issue. In effect the same, small group of officials from each country moved between different fora to get their views across – ILETS, G8, European Union Working Party on police co-operation.

The discussions led to a European Union-FBI 'plan' to get through 'Requirements' to be laid on communications providers to give access to data on production of an 'interception order' and to allow for 'real-time' interception (possibly across a number of countries). The FBI got a new law through in October 1994 and the European Union rushed virtually the same 'Requirements' through on 17 January 1995 (by 'written procedure').

This was just stage one. In 1998 the European Union agencies and the FBI wanted to update the 'Requirements' to cover mobile phones and internet usage but there was a huge public outcry when the document was leaked and the issue was put on 'hold'.⁹ The 'Requirements' however only dealt with specific judicial or administrative orders concerning an individual or a group (in the United Kingdom a warrant signed by the Home Secretary, in other European Union countries usually by a court order) suspected of a *specific* offence. They did not authorise the surveillance of historical data.

When the European Commission proposed, in July 2000, uncontroversial changes to the 1997 European Community Directive on privacy in telecommunications the law enforcement agencies saw their chance. What blocked their access to historical data was the 1997 Directive which said that traffic data (covering phones, mobiles, e-mails, faxes and internet usage) could only be retained for billing purposes (that is, to help the customer) after which it has to be erased. This was usually after three to seven days.

The European Commission, the European Parliament, the European Union Data Protection Commissioner, the European Union's Article 29 Working Party on data protection and a host of civil society groups were opposed to changes which would render the 1997 Directive meaningless. But on 20 September, the European Union Justice and Home Affairs Council adopted a series of measures in response to 11 September. These included access to telecommunications data by law enforcement agencies for the purpose of 'criminal investigations' (not simply terrorism). In December 2001, the European Commission caved in, and then in May the two largest parties in the European Parliament, the PPE (conservatives) and PSE (socialists), also changed their minds and backed the Council's position.

Gone was the privacy protection that traffic data had to be erased and in came a provision allowing European Union member states to adopt laws at national level requiring the retention of traffic data. The hard-won right to privacy in telecommunications was rendered meaningless and the potential surveillance of the whole population of Europe is now on the agenda. Apologists for the changes argued that the new provisions were non-binding and it was up to each member state to adopt laws at a national level. Yet even while the measures were being debated, European Union governments were drafting a binding Framework Decision on the retention of data. They also argue that protections were built in by an express reference to the European Convention on Human Rights – but reference to the Convention provides no additional protection as *all* European Union Directives are automatically subject to it.

This is an example of how the post 11 September ideology has made it much easier to introduce measures governments (and officials) have wanted for a long time.

The European Union state and the creation of unaccountable groups

Post 11 September saw an extraordinary growth in the creation of unaccountable groups of officials and agencies.

The Police Chiefs Operational Task Force (PCOTF) emerged from the Tampere Summit in October 1999, but its legal and constitutional status has never been resolved. It was intended to concentrate on 'three or four top priority organised crime problems', but after 11 September was given a series of operational roles covering intelligence and information exchange; co-operation between national anti-terrorist units, security at airports, border management planning and operations and the co-ordination of para-military police units for European Union Summits and international meetings. When *Statewatch* applied for access to minutes of their meetings, we were told that the Police Chiefs Operational Task Force did not come under the Council of the European Union and therefore the documents could not be supplied.

Security and intelligence chiefs from across the European Union now hold regular meetings. There are no details of their meetings, nor any lines of scrutiny or accountability.

The Spanish Presidency of the Council pushed through a Recommendation allowing the creation of *ad hoc* multinational teams of police and internal security agents (that is, Spain-France-Italy). These teams are explicitly not intended to track down, arrest and charge suspected terrorists – this is the job of the joint investigation teams already agreed under a Framework Decision. It appears these 'teams', in order to 'gather and exchange information', may well follow the infamous precedent set by undercover units in Northern Ireland and Spain.

What we are witnessing, too, is the next stage in the development of the European state, in particular of coercive 'hard' state functions, agencies and practices.[10] The growth of the state in the European Union can be traced from the Trevi era (1976-1993) when policy making (and practical co-operation) was *ad hoc*, intergovernmental and non-binding, through to the Maastricht era (1993-1999) when the previous informal arrangements were formalised and made permanent especially at the policy making level. The Schengen Information System (SIS) went online in March 1995, and Europol became operational in June 1999. But with these two exceptions, it is during the current Amsterdam era (1999 and ongoing) that a whole series of agencies, databases and *ad hoc* groups have emerged as the internal security matrix of the European Union.

Scrutiny of new European Union measures by national parliaments and the European Parliament is simply consultative and their views, when they are sought, are routinely ignored. As to the control and accountability of these new agencies, there is literally no mechanism in place in any parliament. The activities of agencies and the exercise of their unaccountable powers are growing by leaps and bounds. Within years, if not months, the exchange of data on individuals 'suspected' of offences (however minor), or 'suspected' of being an 'illegal' migrant, a visa over-stayer, a 'suspected' protest 'troublemaker' or a request for interception of an individual's or organisations' telecommunications, or a request (under the European arrest warrant) for an individual to be arrested, their person and home searched and items seized and held in detention prior to extradition to another European Union state, will become commonplace. Of course, exceptional abuses of power will end up in the courts or the European

Court of Human Rights, but most will not. We are entering a period when 'self-regulation' (by the agencies of themselves) becomes the norm.

The emerging European Union state is indeed different to the national state, not just because it exercises cross-border powers, but rather because even traditional, and often ineffective, liberal democratic means of control, scrutiny and accountability of state agencies and practices are not in place, nor is there any political will to introduce them.

The Bush letter

When we look back at this period one of the most significant documents will be the letter from Bush to the European Union dated 16 October 2001. This presented a series of 47 demands for European Union-United States co-operation against 'terrorism' – many did not concern 'terrorism' but rather crime and immigration. They included the exchange of telecommunications data, the direct exchange of personal data with Europol, the establishment of common border control policies including data on asylum-seekers, and a new category of 'inadmissibles' to be refused entry by the United States and the European Union.[11]

Since 16 October 2001, there have been dozens of meetings between European Union and United States officials in both continents, and United States (and Canadian) officials are sitting in on numerous European Union working party meetings on immigration and asylum, standard forms for reporting, transit plans (whereby the United States deports people to Asia and Africa via European Union airports), border management, Europol, policing, cybercrime and drugs.

Despite the widely reported differences between the European Union and the United States on how to prosecute the 'war on terrorism' at the international level, we are seeing in practice an entirely new level of European Union-United States co-operation on internal security. This represents a partial shift from informal trans-governmentalism (meetings in secret international fora) to the formalisation of co-operation between the European Union and the United States. We are witnessing the creation of a 'northern axis' with a common internal security policy. The United States is, in effect, the sixteenth member of the European Union.[12]

Targets of the new ideology

The emerging ideology utterly blurs the distinction between terrorism and resistance to oppression and political dissent, between resistance/liberation struggles against authoritarian and undemocratic regimes and plain terrorist groups, and between self-defence by protestors against attack, or self-defence by migrants of their local communities against racist and police incursions. Moreover, this new 'anti-terrorist' ideology has quickly permeated not just the language but also the concrete proposals from the European Union.

Translated into practice we can see the first two groups of targets of the new internal security strategy of the European Union state: protests and protestors (see above) and refugees and asylum-seekers, visitors on visas, plus resident, settled, third country nationals. All are potential terrorists or 'supporters' of terrorism, whether 'actively or passively'. This means their international movements have to be recorded (whether via the new visa database or as air passengers). Asylum applications have to be vetted by the security agencies to check for any connection with alleged terrorists. Selected groups of third country nationals have been targeted, checked and 'profiled'.

Under the guise of combating terrorism, the rights of resident third country nationals are to be weakened. Whereas the original draft European Union proposal on the rights of third country nationals in the European Union said that a criminal offence would not be grounds for removing residence rights, now this has changed so that a criminal (not terrorist) offence can lead to the deportation of whole families.

Thus, the logic of the 'terrorism' ideology brings with it a new form of institutionalised racism in the European Union. A racism based on a move from multiculturalism (communities of many races coexisting) to monoculturalism (white, Western, values now have to be adopted by migrants through so-called 'integration' measures) and where:

> European anti-terrorist laws, adopted post 11 September, are breeding a culture of suspicion against Muslims and people of Middle-Eastern appearance, who are increasingly treated in the same way as were 'enemy aliens' during the First and Second World Wars[13]

Just a temporary aberration?

I have just described a few of the dozens of new measures introduced post 11 September. It can be asked whether all the measures are entirely new or were in the pipeline anyway – the answer is that some were, some were not, but most not in the form in which they have emerged.

Are these developments simply temporary? Will the demonisation of protestors, refugees and asylum-seekers and others come to an end and the old tolerance and democratic values, however imperfect, re-assert themselves? Is what is happening simply like a big stone dropped into a pond and the large ripples get smaller and smaller and finally it is smooth again – everything is back to normal.

The answer is no. Something much bigger is happening. A.Sivanandan, Director of the Institute of Race Relations, says:

> Globalisation has set up a monolithic economic system; September 11 threatens to engender a monolithic political culture. Together, they spell the end of civil society.

He is absolutely right, we are seeing a 'sea change' – the forging of a new global hegemony similar but quite different to that of the Cold War era. The European Union is not immune from this new ideology but rather is helping to shape it. European Union governments have colluded in the outrageous bombing and aftermath in Afghanistan, and some are doing likewise in Iraq. The 'legitimacy', the tone, of the new ideology may differ between the European Union and the United States, but its effect is the same. In each the fight against 'terrorism' and the consequential re-drawing of the boundaries between the demands for security and the preservation of civil liberties and peoples' rights is presented, reported on, and largely accepted as defending the common interest, the common good, the interests of all.

It is also important to situate the new ideology in the European Union's political landscape, because there is a dreadful conjuncture between new repressive measures post 11 September and the rise of racist and fascist political parties across Europe.[14] There was a time when there were 12 social democratic governments as against three from the right, but that time is long gone. Now nine are from the right or extreme-right, and six from the centre to so-called centre-left (United Kingdom, Germany, Sweden, Finland, Belgium and Greece). Not only has the European Union as a whole moved to the right but, in reaction to the rise of racist parties in electoral politics, the social democrats have demonstrably shifted to the right, too, on immigration, migrants' rights and mono-culturalism. The racists (and fascists), rather than being disowned, have found their views embraced by European Union governments in order to retain power.

Is it possible for a 'democracy' to slide into lawlessness? Most of the checks and balances laid down, and the role of the courts, are geared to ensuring that the 'law' is properly implemented. But what if the new laws themselves are antithetical to democratic values? The checks and balances are still in place, and the courts too, but these cannot be guarantors of the legitimacy of excessive laws – that is, laws which remove basic rights.

One by one the historical norms of the liberal-democratic culture are being undermined or abolished. The next in line may be the European Court of Human Rights itself. The Council of Europe has started the process of revising the 1950 Convention – which could not be happening at a worse time. One of the critical provisions for the rights of refugees is Article 3 on Prohibition of Torture which says:

> No one shall be subjected to torture or to inhuman or degrading treatment or punishment

A number of leading European Union governments (including the United Kingdom) are considering backing a proposal to remove the words: 'or to inhuman or degrading treatment or punishment'.

In previous periods of history we have seen draconian measures put through at the national level but, in my view, we have never seen such an assault on peoples' rights and democratic standards.[15] Each new measure, viewed on its own, may seem an aberration, but a whole host of changes as part of an ongoing continuum constitutes a shift of enormous proportions.

There is another, hidden, issue – that of collusion, active or passive. Governments, ministers and officials who are bringing in these sweeping changes do so consciously and are therefore responsible for their actions. Police officers, prison guards, immigration border officials, para-military police units, undercover agents feel no need to question the consequences of their actions – they are simply following lawful orders. But there is collusion, too, by many others. Officials who disagree but who keep silent for fear of their jobs, journalists who simply report press releases and 'spin' as fact, and so on. And in the wider civil society, too, there is a collusion, a collusion of silence and inaction. Many can see that you cannot defend 'democracy' by destroying it, but choose to stay silent and get on with their comfortable daily lives – what is happening does not affect them.

If we are to restore democracy and liberties each of us has to find our own form of resistance. This may be by writing letters, publishing critical academic articles, tracking, monitoring and publicising what is happening, building coalitions of resistance and through protests in the streets and cities of Europe.

References

1. This is not to argue that there has ever been a 'golden age' when 'liberal democracy' was in place. Rather it is say that from this point onwards liberal democratic culture was in retreat.
2. Wilton Park paper 120, HMSO, 1996.
3. Parliamentarianism at its worst argues that having been elected governments have the right to govern unhindered by the views of their people on particular issues.
4. An *acquis* is an accumulated list of adopted measures/policies.
5. The Amsterdam Treaty came into effect in May 1999.
6. Nor were researchers from within the EU allowed access to hundreds of documents assessing the 'state of play' in the negotiations with the applicant countries. Access we were told could impede ongoing negotiations and undermine the efforts of the EU.
7. Their formal adoption was delayed by national parliamentary scrutiny reserves. The Framework Decision on combating terrorism came into effect on 23 June 2002 and the Framework Decision on the European arrest warrant on 13 June 2002.
8. At the time of writing a number of requests (eg: from the USA and France) for the extradition of terrorist 'suspects', post 11 September, have been rejected by British courts because the requesting state failed to provide acceptable evidence to support its demand.
9. Interception of telecommunications Council Draft Resolution in relation to new technologies, ENFOPOL 98, 10951/98, 3.9.98.
10. While it is certainly true that theories on the national 'state' cannot simply be applied to the EU most academic theory suggests there is no such thing as a European 'state'. Typically the EU would be described as: 'a non-state polity with postnational governance arrangements and an indeterminate form', Jo Shaw in 'Voices, spaces and processes in constitutionalism', Blackwells, 2000. Others concentrate on the views and opinions of the 'actors' (officials, officers, agents) rather than structures to offer an explanation of the EU's development – which is not very productive as state 'actors', at national or the European level, very rarely comprehend the totality in which they operate.

11. On the basis of this an EU working party has proposed that 'inadmissibles' should include those 'flagged' by NATO, the World Trade Organisation and other international bodies.
12. By sitting in on EU preparatory working parties US officials are in a position to exercise an unseen and unaccountable influence on EU policy-making and practices. This is in addition to cooperation on the whole host of broad measures set out in the Bush letter and subsequent meetings.
13. See: 'Racism: the hidden cost of September 11', by Liz Fekete (*Spokesman 75*).
14. This is not to say that racist politics are the preserve of overtly racist parties. Ever since the mid-1980s at least many EU governments and the Council of the European Union have fuelled racism by their rhetoric and practices.
15. For example, the UK's temporary Prevention of Terrorism Act in 1974 which still lives on today in the Terrorism Act 2000.

Greetings from the NUJ

The union that fights for press freedom and trade union rights

Jeremy Dear
General Secretary

George MacIntyre
President

On Twain, Lincoln, Imperialist Wars and the Weather

Kurt Vonnegut

Kurt Vonnegut recently delivered the annual Clemens Lecture at the Mark Twain House in Hartford, Connecticut, an edited version of which we present here.

First things first: I want it clearly understood that this mustache I'm wearing is my father's mustache. I should have brought his photograph. My big brother Bernie, now dead, a physical chemist who discovered that silver iodide can sometimes make it snow or rain, he wore it, too.

Speaking of weather: Mark Twain said some readers complained that there wasn't enough weather in his stories. So he wrote some weather, which they could insert wherever they thought it would help some.

Mark Twain was said to have shed a tear of gratitude and incredulousness when honored for his writing by Oxford University in England. And I should shed a tear, surely, having been asked at the age of eighty, and because of what I myself have written, to speak under the auspices of the sacred Mark Twain House here in Hartford.

What other American landmark is as sacred to me as the Mark Twain House? The Lincoln Memorial in Washington, DC. Mark Twain and Abraham Lincoln were country boys from Middle America, and both of them made the American people laugh at themselves and appreciate really important, really moral jokes.

I note that construction has stopped here in Hartford of a Mark Twain Museum – behind the carriage house of the Mark Twain House at 351 Farmington Avenue.

Work persons have been sent home from that site because American 'Conservatives,' as they call themselves, on Wall Street and at the head of so many of our corporations, have stolen a major fraction of our private savings, have ruined investors and employees by means of fraud and outright piracy.

Shock and awe.

And now, having installed themselves as our Federal Government, or taken control of it from outside, they have squandered our public treasury and then some. They have created a public debt of such appalling magnitude that our descendents, for whom we had such high hopes, will come into this world as poor as church mice.

Shock and awe.

What are the Conservatives doing with all the money and power that used to belong to all of us? They are telling us to be absolutely terrified, and to run around in circles like chickens with their heads cut off. But they will save us. They are making us take off our shoes at airports. Can anybody here think of a more hilarious practical joke than that one?

Smile, America. You're on Candid Camera.

And they have turned loose a myriad of our high tech weapons, each one costing more than a hundred high schools, on a Third World country, in order to shock and awe human beings like us, like Adam and Eve, between the Tigris and Euphrates Rivers.

The other day I asked the former Yankees pitcher Jim Bouton what he thought of our great victory over Iraq, and he said, 'Mohammed Ali *versus* Mr. Rogers.'

What are Conservatives? They are people who will move Heaven and Earth, if they have to, who will ruin a company or a country or a planet, to prove to us and themselves that they are superior to everybody else, except for their pals. They take good care of their pals, keep them out of jail – and so on.

Conservatives are crazy as bedbugs. They are bullies.

Shock and awe.

Class war? You bet.

They have proved their superiority to admirers of Abraham Lincoln and Mark Twain and Jesus of Nazareth by, with an able assist from television, making inconsequential our protests against their war.

What has happened to us? We have suffered a technological calamity. Television is now our form of government.

On what grounds did we protest their war? I could name many, but I need name only one, which is common sense.

Be that as it may, construction of the Mark Twain Museum will sooner or later be resumed. And I, the son and grandson of Indiana architects, seize this opportunity to suggest a feature which I hope will be included in the completed structure, words to be chiseled into the capstone over the main entrance.

Here is what I think would be fun to put up there, and Mark Twain loved fun more than anything. I have tinkered with something famous he said, which is:

'Be good and you will be lonesome.' That is from 'Following the Equator.' OK?

So envision what a majestic front entrance the Mark Twain Museum will have someday. And imagine that these words have been chiseled into the noble capstone and painted gold:

BE GOOD AND YOU WILL BE LONESOME MOST PLACES, BUT NOT HERE, NOT HERE.

One of the most humiliated and heartbroken pieces Twain ever wrote was about the slaughter of one hundred Moro men, women and children by our soldiers during our liberation of the people of the Philippines after the Spanish American

War. Our brave commander was Leonard Wood, who now has a fort named after him. Fort Leonard Wood.

What did Abraham Lincoln have to say about such American Imperialist wars? Those are wars which, on one noble pretext or another, actually aim to increase the natural resources and pools of tame labor available to the richest Americans who have the best political connections.

And it is almost always a mistake to mention Abraham Lincoln in a speech about something or somebody else. He always steals the show. I am about to quote him.

Lincoln was only a Congressman when he said in 1848 what I am about to echo. He was heartbroken and humiliated by our war on Mexico, which had never attacked us.

We were making California our own, and a lot of other people and properties, and doing it as though butchering Mexican soldiers who were only defending their homeland against invaders weren't murder.

What other stuff besides California? Well, Texas, New Mexico, Utah, Nevada, Arizona, and parts of Colorado and Wyoming.

The person Congressman Lincoln had in mind when he said what he said was James Polk, our President at the time. Abraham Lincoln said of Polk, his President, our armed forces' Commander and Chief:

> Trusting to escape scrutiny by fixing the public gaze upon the exceeding brightness of military glory, that attractive rainbow that rises in showers of blood – that serpent's eye, that charms to destroy, he plunged into war.'

Holy smokes! I almost said, 'Holy shit!' And I thought I was a writer!

Do you know we actually captured Mexico City during the Mexican War? Why isn't that a national holiday? And why isn't the face of James Polk up on Mount Rushmore, along with Ronald Reagan's?

What made Mexico so evil back in the 1840's, well before our Civil War, is that slavery was illegal there. Remember the Alamo?

My great grandfather's name was Clemens Vonnegut. Small world, small world.

This piquant coincidence is not a fabrication.

Clemens Vonnegut called himself a 'Freethinker,' an antique word for Humanist. He was a hardware merchant in Indianapolis.

So, 120 years ago, say, there was one man who was both Clemens and Vonnegut. I would have liked being such a person a lot. I only wish I could have been such a person tonight.

I claim no blood relationship with Samuel Clemens of Hannibal, Missouri. 'Clemens,' as a first name, is, I believe, like the name 'Clementine,' derived from the adjective 'clement.' To be clement is to be lenient and compassionate, or, in the case of weather, perfectly heavenly.

So there's weather again.

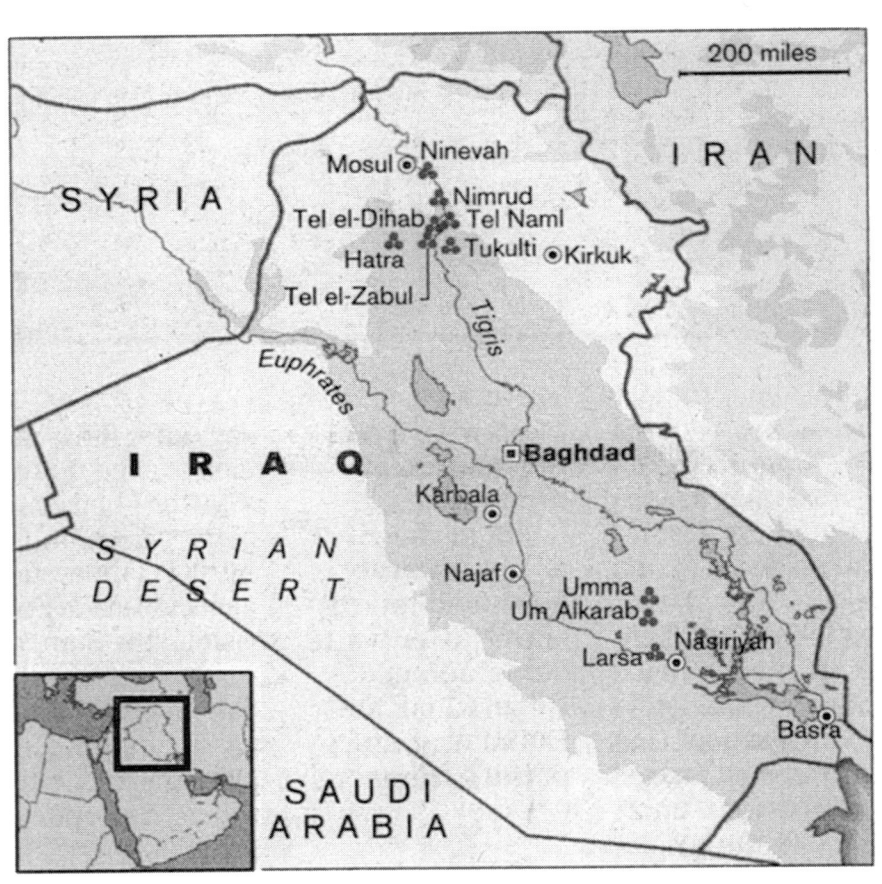

Raiders of the Lost Iraq

Robert Fisk

The distinguished writer, journalist and Middle East correspondent of the London Independent *newspaper reports how, under the noses of the Anglo-American occupying forces, the priceless heritage of ancient Sumeria is being pillaged to order for Western collectors. Robert Fisk is the author of* Pity the Nation.

It looks as though a B-52 has carpet-bombed the city called Mother of Scorpions. I clamber around 20ft craters and try to recognise one of the greatest cities of civilisation. But the thieves have done their work. They have broken or stolen everything. For 10 square miles, they have dug and smashed and gouged into the ancient earth, and destroyed the priceless heritage of Mesopotamia. The Sumerian palaces, the temple walls, the great pillars, oil lamps and giant pots and delicately patterned plates and dishes, all have been smashed to bits.

After three hours walking ankle-deep through the shards and fragments of dishes and handmade bricks, I found a tall, slender pot of green clay. One of our ancestors – one of my ancestors, I couldn't help thinking – had worked on this pot more than 4,000 years ago. There was a slight indent on the bottom where his hand might have slipped, a long graceful neck up which his fingers must have passed many times, and then a thin lip at the top, sufficiently narrow that the potter must have brought his two hands so close that they might have been in prayer. It was then that I realised that the top of this beautiful thing was cracked, and only when I lifted it gently in my own hands did I realise the obscenity of the looter's work. This perfect, unbroken work of art, this treasure from the people who invented writing – who gave us the first laws and the calendar and mathematics and the wheel and the great epic of Gilgamesh – had been cast aside by the looters, tossed carelessly down a slope of sand and stone and snapped in two.

There were other plates and vessels lying smashed around me. The thief who had been digging here was looking for early Sumerian antiquities – the collectors of America, Europe, the Middle East and Japan want the pots and statues and jewels of 5,500 years ago, not the heritage of 2000BC – and so everything above the earliest layers of civilisation had to be thrown away. The robber probably took no more than 60 seconds to hurl away these pots and plates made 2000 years before Christ. It was the Sumerians who created our own concept of time, dividing it into units of 60. Alas, the looter's only concession to history was the empty packet of cheap Iraqi cigarettes that lay beside the wreckage. Printed on it was a harp and the name of the manufacturer: 'Sumer'.

The Mother of Scorpions – 'Um Alkarab' – is in an area called Jokhr, the name of the nearest modern-day village some 40 miles northwest of Nasiriyah, although there is nothing modern about it. The clay houses, with their wooden beams poking from the walls, their gatepost designs, and the small, intensely worked fields, are almost identical to those of the Sumerians who learnt, perhaps 7,000 years ago, to irrigate this land with the canals and ditches that brought the waters of the Tigris river to the desert. The canals are still there. 'Saddam dried all of them and dammed the water,' one of the villagers told me. 'Then, when the Americans started bombing, the waters flowed back for the first time in years.'

It's about the only good thing the Americans have done for this ancient landscape. For the mass looting and destruction of the great Sumerian sites in the two months since the Americans 'liberated' Iraq is likely to prove one of the most terrible cultural crimes of recent history, far more shameful than the calculated acts of robbery and vandalism at Baghdad's Museum of Archaeology in April. Even now, this act of mass barbarism has scarcely been noted, let alone understood. Nimrud and Ninevah – the home of King Sennacherib – Hatra, Tel Naml, Tukulti, Tel el-Zabul, Larsa, Tel el-Jbeit, Tel el-Dihab and Kulal-Jabr have all been substantially looted and, in some cases, destroyed. American troops put a guard on Ninevah and Hatra – but only after the thieves had run amok there.

We may weep over Dresden. But over the past eight weeks, the extent of cultural loss in the land where civilisation began cannot be measured in tears. Part of ourselves has been destroyed, part of our humanity. We had been warned. And we did nothing. It is the greatest untold story of this latest war in Iraq.

There are tears aplenty at Um Alkarab, many of them running down the face of Eqbal Qazem, the 35-year-old deputy director of the Museum of Antiquities in Nasiriyah. She it was who prevented the looters of 1991 from thieving the antiquities of her museum during the great Shiite 'intifada' against Saddam's rule – the rebellion encouraged by President George Bush Senior and then betrayed when the Americans failed to come to the aid of the insurgents. As shooting broke out in the streets of Nasiriyah, she first fled the museum and then – fearing for the treasures she had grown to love – returned to sew the earrings and jewels from all the museum cases into her own clothes and then took a taxi to Baghdad. The government later rewarded her for her courage – then posted an ignorant Baath party apparatchik to run the museum and make her life a misery.

Twelve years ago, she risked her life for the heritage of the Sumerians. Now, she was stumbling around the wreckage of their history, her shoulders shaking, the tears dropping off her face into the hot sand. 'How can I do anything but cry,' she says. 'This is one of the greatest tragedies to archaeology.' When I find a 3,000-year-old oil lamp – perfect only a few weeks ago but now broken neatly in half – she takes it lovingly in her hands and runs her fingers round the bright red bowl. Then she throws it, choking on her tears, into the sand. 'We can take nothing from this site – it is not allowed,' she says, and then laughs bitterly at such morality. The staff of the Baghdad museums must abide by the old Baathist rules – take nothing from the site lest they be accused of theft – while the real thieves, the big-time pros with order-books to complete from Switzerland or New York or London, take out the treasures by the truckload.

And I mean truckload. The tyre-marks of heavy lorries run right up to the stones of Um Alkarab. In the neighbouring city of Umma, seven square miles of antiquities destroyed just like Um Alkarab, the thieves are still at work. In fact, I walked right up to them as they sat outside their tents, strung out between amateur piles of excavations. They joke with the armed guards who are supposed to protect the site – and whom I increasingly suspect of sharing in the theft – and laugh when one of the local tribesmen, holding a Kalashnikov rifle, shouts across the wreckage: 'We do not come to harm you.' The harm has already been done, not to them or us, but to that which belongs to us all under the soil.

'I don't know who these people were,' one of the thieves tells me, grinning beneath his bright red kuffiah and holding up a large fragment of mid-Sumerian pottery, decorated with a clay band of rope. 'I just dig down and take what I find and sell it.' But that's not all he does. At Um Alkarab, there was a palace, its walls inlaid with bricks, each brick containing the mark of the thumb and forefinger of its maker. They formed a façade to the palace, along with the nearby temple. Greedy for hidden jewels, the robbers have torn the bricks from the wall, ripping down the wall itself, destroying almost the entire palace. Nearby lies part of a large pot and in it some human remains many thousands of years old, two pieces of bone as white as ivory. One of the guards picks them up, snorts with derision and throws them into the sand. I pick them up and put them back in the fragment of pot before realising the truth; that it's the life these people created – the life they gave to us, not their bones – that is sacred.

Joanne Farchakh, a Lebanese archaeologist who is conducting an exhaustive study of the mass post-war theft of Iraq's cultural history for the French magazine *Archéologia*, and who puts her arm around Eqbal Qzem's shoulders when her friend cries, believes that no archeological destruction on this scale has occurred for at least 1,000 years. 'These cities are among the most important in Sumerian civilisation, and Um Alkarab and Umma are now effectively gone,' she says. 'They have been destroyed. There was some looting before this war – in museums during the 1991 uprising against Saddam and, for example, at Ninevah – where thieves stole pieces of a decorated wall.'

One piece of that wall was later found by British police – it was on its way to a collector in Israel – and later returned to Iraq. But three weeks ago, the thieves returned en masse to take the rest of the wall, and tore it to bits. 'You have to understand what these collectors are like,' Farchakh says. 'They want missing parts of their collection. They have, say, Akkadian pottery and Babylonian artefacts, and they have late- and mid-Sumerian, but they want early Sumerian so they put this on order – to complete their collections. The thieves who come here have order-books to complete. They hack their way down to the early Sumerian period and destroy everything that is above it to fulfil their order. The same thing happened in the Baghdad Museum. The thieves there were looking for heads of 2,000-year-old statues, so they smashed the statues on the floor to get the heads off. They wanted heads of around 300BC. One of the statues simply broke into pieces.'

Iraqi archaeologists express gloomy praise for Saddam Hussein's efforts to preserve the heritage of Iraq – or at least that part of the heritage that he didn't loot for himself – and remember with some satisfaction the hanging of nine men in Mosul in 1998 for attempting to smuggle archaeological remains out of the country. As war appeared inevitable last autumn, archaeologists in both Iraq and the United States did their best to safeguard the cultural treasures of Mesopotamia. In Baghdad, museum staff began moving gold and jewellery to Central Bank vaults where the so-called 'Treasure of Nimrud' had already been stored, and transferred other museum artefacts to a secret storage vault in the Mansur district of the city. In Washington, American experts on the archaeology of Mesopotamia, including McGuire Gibson of the University of Chicago's Oriental Institute, held their now-famous meeting with Pentagon planners to warn of the dangers to the cultural heritage of the land they were about to invade. The Pentagon was told about the vast Sumerian sites in the south of the country, including those around Nasiriyah – the same sites I saw last week just after their destruction.

The Bush administration's reaction was somewhere beneath contempt. After the White House spokesman Ari Fleischer tried to shirk off responsibility for the looting by claiming that it was 'a reaction to oppression', and after the Secretary of Defence Donald Rumsfeld's shameful response, 'Stuff happens!', the most meretricious remark came from Brigadier General Vincent Brooks, the spokesman for US Central Command in Qatar. 'I don't think that anyone anticipated that the riches of Iraq would be looted by the Iraqi people,' he said. This was preposterous. The looting of 1991 showed just how far mass robbery might go – and the idea that 'the Iraqi people' were responsible for the theft of Iraq's treasures was almost racist. Weren't the foreign buyers – including US buyers – implicated in this cultural genocide?

Besides, the Americans had no reason to claim that they had no warning. Quite apart from the Pentagon meeting, there were numerous articles in the international press about the dangers of looting. An article in the *International Herald Tribune* on 8 March warned how 'looters dig up archaeological sites' in Iraq, adding presciently that 'archaeological sites in the area urgently require armed protection if a conflict is to break out'. A report in *The Independent on Sunday* two months earlier, on 12 January, recounted the history of archaeological excavation in Iraq, and warned of the dangers to its national treasures in the event of hostilities. But General Brooks' remark is even more preposterous in the light of a remarkable article entitled 'Threat to Civilisation' that appeared in the American armed forces' own newspaper, *Stars and Stripes*, on 23 March – five clear days after the Anglo-American invasion began.

The newspaper, read by every American serving soldier, sailor and airman, reported McGuire Gibson's warning that 'losses could occur after the bombing stops, recalling the looting of up to 4,000 objects from Iraq's cities after the [1991] Persian Gulf War', and went on to itemise the list of 'priceless artefacts' in the Baghdad Museum, including '40,000-year-old stone and flint objects, 5,000-year-old cylinder seals, and 4,500-year-old gold-leaf earrings once buried with Sumerian princesses'. There were other references to the risks of looting in the article. Yet despite all this, General Brooks claimed that the looting could not have been 'anticipated'?

The story of the museum looting took the first shine off the Bush-Blair 'victory' in the war; sadly, the failure to find weapons of mass destruction is sabotaging their boasts far more damagingly than the destruction of civilisation's birthplace. Ever since *The Independent* and a French TV crew entered the Baghdad museum early on 11 April – only hours after the looters had fled with the sacred vase of Warca and the Akkadian Basitki statue, and hundreds of other priceless treasures – the Americans have been trying to account for their abysmal failure to safeguard the cultural relics of the nation they were supposedly liberating. Even then, it was 16 April – six days after the looting – before a US tank platoon turned up to guard the museum.

After I had crunched over the smashed pottery in the museum storage-room on 11 April, I compared the looting to the cultural genocide of the Second World War. But after visiting the Sumerian sites of southern Iraq – where infinitely more treasures were almost certainly discovered and then sold off to foreign collectors – I'm inclined to place the losses on a more epic scale, something proportionate to the burning of the great library of Alexandria in antiquity.

The Americans have desperately tried to square up their moral position by sending into Baghdad squads of FBI men, CIA agents and army intelligence boys to hunt down the missing artefacts. NYPD cops and United Airlines managers who are reservists for the intelligence corps are now reading the epic of Gilgamesh and learning how Semitic civilisation succeeded the Sumerians, founding the city of Babylon and the Assyrian capital of Ninevah. 'Before I was posted to this investigation, I couldn't even spell "Iraq",' one of the intelligence men admitted to me last week. And the Americans have been trying to make things look good, at least for themselves.

Their most recent report states that museum staff left the building on 8 April after which 'US forces became engaged in intense combat with Iraqi forces that fought from the museum grounds... It was during this period that the looting took place, ending by 12 April when some staff returned. The keys to the museum, previously locked away in a director's safe, have never been found'. In fact, the looting had ended by early on 11 April, when I entered the building. Joanne Farchakh, the Lebanese archaeologist, remains convinced – as do many of the US investigators – that this was an 'inside' job. Indeed, she suspects that many of the items stolen – especially the 94cm Warca vase with its illustrations of the daily rituals in the temple of the Gods – may well have been ordered by international collectors before the war even began.

'They are so selfish, these collectors,' she says. 'If they have the Warca vase, they can never show it – they can't, because they'd be arrested. It's like having the Mona Lisa. They'll just have to put it in a cave and go and check on it from time to time. This is incredibly selfish behaviour – the collectors are very selfish. But they are buying and when you buy, you send the message, 'More!' That's why the Sumerian sites are now destroyed.'

Significantly, the primary goal of the US law-enforcement team was not criminal prosecution. Thieves apprehended in Baghdad with figurines, shards of pottery or beads are not prosecuted. The Americans take the artefacts and let the robbers go home. Which means, of course, that the dealers in London and Geneva and New York, and the squalid but wealthy groups of international collectors – their life made even safer by Britain's attempts to water down anti-smuggling legislation in Brussels – have very little to worry about.

Two weeks ago, more than a month after the looting of the museum, Colonel Matthew Bogdanos, the senior US investigating officer, complained that his men were hampered by the museum's 'manual and incomplete record-keeping system' and the widespread belief that the museum was part of Saddam Hussein's Baath party. 'After the [US] team located boxes of priceless books and manuscripts in a western Baghdad bomb shelter, it attempted to return them to the museum,' Bogdanos said. But after local residents objected to their transfer back to the museum until it was under new management, 'the team received inventories for the boxes and agreed to leave them locked in the shelter, protected by a 24-hour neighbourhood watch'.

There was nothing imaginary about the residents' fears. Last week, for example, a shouting match broke out in the museum between Iraqi executives and junior staff. The cause was as simple as it was frightening. The management are Baath party appointees and under Saddam's regime they wrote regular reports on the junior staff for the Iraqi intelligence services. Today, they are still refusing to let the staff see these reports – even though one curator believes that a report written about him led to his brother's execution by hanging. The management refused to let him see the paper and identify the signature. When the staff approached the US forces at the museum, they declined to intervene.

For their part, museum officials refused to disclose the whereabouts of another 'secret' storage location to the Americans 'until a new government in Iraq is established and US forces leave the country'. The Americans had to be content with an inventory of the items that they were not allowed to see. Colonel Bogdanos lists nine of the 42 major pieces stolen from the museum's public galleries as recovered, but among the 33 still missing are the Warca vase and the Basitki statue. Fifteen other pieces were damaged, including the magnificent Golden Harp of Ur, although its golden head had earlier been removed to a bank vault. Of 2,100 excavation-site jars, vessels and pottery shards stolen from storage rooms, 800 were recovered. But, as another US intelligence officer told me last week, 'don't get carried away when we say we've found another '15 pieces'. People think we're talking about 15 statues. But the 'piece' may only be part of a pot the size of your nail'. In temporary storage rooms, only 12 out of 150 pieces have been recovered.

The Americans do claim to have discovered evidence that Iraqi fighters used the museum in their last battle with US troops at the end of the war. The US team says it found rocket-propelled grenade parts, an ammunition box and a cartridge clip near a storage-room window slit, and say that grenades were fired at them from the roof of the children's museum. Blood from a dead or dying fighter was also found in the storage room. Certainly, there are Iraqi slit trenches still in the grounds of the museum where I found AK-47 cartridges when I entered on 11 April. The thieves, the Americans claim, appeared to have arrived after the fighters had left.

And it was their possession of museum keys that provided them with their prize. In one storage room, according to Colonel Bogdanos, 'the thieves had keys that were previously hidden in the museum. These keys were to storage cabinets in that room that contained thousands of Greek, Roman and Hellenistic coins. Ironically, the thieves appear to have dropped the keys in one of the boxes. After frantically and unsuccessfully searching for them in the dark and throwing the boxes in every direction, they left without opening any of the cabinets'.

No one in Iraq, and few academics in America, doubt that the US bears a heavy responsibility for the destruction of Iraq's cultural heritage – even before the discovery of the mass pillage of the great Sumerian archeological sites that should provoke an even more passionate outcry than the looting of the Baghdad museum. International law, however, is vague about the duties of an occupying power. The Fourth Hague Convention of 1907 states that 'pillage is formally forbidden'. This became part of the 1949 Geneva Convention, but the Geneva Protocols – which contain a paragraph on the 'Protection of Cultural Property in the Event of Armed Conflict' – was never signed by the US.

In any event, the pillage of Iraq – which is still going on under the eyes of the Anglo-American occupying power – is having a strange and powerful effect. When the market is glutted with stolen artefacts, prices usually fall. But today, they are rising sharply for Sumerian, Akkadian and Babylonian treasures. 'So much of Mesopotamian history is now flooding the markets, that collectors want more,' says Joanne Farchakh. 'They are voracious. The international markets hide these people from the law. Iraq's soil is rich with these treasures that are being stolen.' And the occupying powers are doing almost nothing about it. Why should they? They don't have to worry about the ancient city of Umma any more, nor the city called Mother of Scorpions. Because they no longer exist.

By kind permission of *The Independent* ©, 5 June 2003

The Price of Oil

Zhores A. Medvedev

*Dr Medvedev's new book,
The Unknown Stalin, will
be published by I.B.Tauris
in the autumn.*

At the beginning of 2002, the increase in the world output of oil nearly ceased, having reached 3.4 billion tonnes a year. By itself, this fact was not unexpected. Scientific research into petroleum resources did not promise endless growth. But the majority of the prognoses of the last ten years expected output to peak in 2006 at 3.7 billion tonnes. The earlier and lower maximum was, however, easily explained. It was a result of the restrictive sanctions on the output of oil in Iraq, imposed by the United Nations in 1991. Under these sanctions, Iraq was compelled to reduce the production and export of oil by 700 million barrels a year. This amounted to just 2.5 per cent of world output. But this lost projected growth in oil production over four years would cause very sharp shortages, first and foremost for the United States.

The United States, which consumed 26 per cent of world oil production in 2001, suffered most acutely from the increasing energy deficit.

Hostages of prosperity

In 2000, the United States consumed 790 million tonnes of oil. The greater part of this, 675 million tonnes, was for transport. Americans consume a third of the world's energy for transport. This amounts to 18 barrels per person per year, more than twice as much as Europe, Japan or Australia, and thirty times as much as China.

For 15 years, from 1986 to 1999, the price of petrol in the United States was low and stable at between 25 and 30 cents a litre. There, motorists pay almost no tax on petrol, so that fluctuations in the price of petrol and diesel fuel depend almost directly on changes in the price of crude oil. In Europe and Japan the purchase of liquid fuel incurs very high taxes. In Britain, for example, petrol costs 80 pence a litre (one dollar twenty cents), but three-quarters of this is tax.

Cheap petrol in the United States allows

Americans to buy new houses and settle further and further away from the cities where they work. Inevitably, this lengthens the daily journey to work and to the shopping centres. Children have to be taken to school on special buses. By 2000, there were 132 million private cars in the United States, and 79 million goods vehicles and buses. During the past 15 years, the transportation of goods by road in the United States increased twice over, reaching two trillion kilometre-tonnes. This significantly exceeds the volume of goods transported in all the countries of the European Union, together with those of Eastern Europe. Since 1997, expenditure on transport has become the largest item in the budgets of the families of middle America, exceeding spending on housing and food. According to published statistics, an 'average American' travels twice as far a year and consumes four times as much petrol as an 'average German'.

The unexpected doubling of the price of oil in the second half of 2000, to between 30 and 35 dollars a barrel, caused a jump in the price of petrol in the United States to 50 to 56 cents a litre. This rapid rise in transport costs hit the United States economy hard. During the next year the value of shares on the general index of the New York Stock Exchange fell from 11,700 to 7,800, while shares on the high technology index fell to a quarter of their former value. This was the beginning of the recession which did not respond to the usual measures of cuts in interest rates and reductions in taxes. To these problems was added the rapid rise in the trade and budgetary deficits. Judging by the dynamics of prices on the world market, a new 'oil shock' had begun, although there was no war in the Middle East. Three previous 'shocks', in 1973, 1980 and 1991, were associated with wars and therefore considered unavoidable. The jump in 2000 was blamed on OPEC's economic policy.

The political price of oil

World export prices of copper, steel or coal are determined by free competition of producers and exporters within the confines of a market economy. The world export prices of oil depend on the decisions of the Organisation of Petroleum Exporting Countries (OPEC). This cartel was established in 1960 by five countries: Saudi Arabia, Iran, Iraq, Kuwait and Venezuela, especially to halt free competition between exporters, and to guarantee higher prices for oil and better profits for oil producing countries. In 1960, the OPEC countries produced about 35 per cent of world oil output. A further 35 per cent or so was produced in the United States. The rest of the world, including the Soviet Union, accounted for the remaining 30 per cent. In 1960, the United States was not an importer but an exporter of oil, and the increases in world prices for oil did not alarm Americans at all. At that time, the Soviet Union exported oil only to Eastern Europe, and not at world prices, but denominated in roubles. In 1960, general world production of oil was about one billion tonnes a year. During the following years, OPEC grew to include Qatar, Indonesia, Libya, the Arab Emirates, Algeria, Gabon and Equador. In 1973, when OPEC took a political decision to double the export price of oil and to embargo deliveries of oil to countries which supported Israel in the Arab-Israeli war, the main victims appeared to be the United States and Western

Europe. In 1973, the United States economy imported almost 30 per cent of its oil. Western Europe imported all its liquid fuel. The 'oil shock' caused a deep recession in all the western countries. For the Soviet Union, by contrast, OPEC's decision turned out to be a stroke of luck. The vast oil resources of Western Siberia had already been opened up, but the cost of transportation to the European part of the country was prohibitive. At that time, the Soviet Union did not manufacture pipes of sufficient diameter to construct a viable pipeline. Pipes for the internal pipelines from the Caspian region were purchased in the United States.

The economic crisis in Europe changed the oil situation. The Federal Republic of Germany began to finance the construction of an oil pipeline from Siberia to central Europe. Industry in the Federal Republic supplied large diameter steel pipes and high capacity cladding on credit. Future repayments of credit were guaranteed not in money but supplies of oil. The Soviet Union soon became the most significant exporter of oil, second in volume terms after Saudi Arabia.

The war between Iraq and Iran, which lasted from 1980 to 1988, and then Iraq's occupation of Kuwait in 1990, greatly weakened OPEC's political and economic position. These were wars between member countries of the organisation. In these circumstances, it was impossible to regulate oil output effectively and control export prices. Competition broke out between OPEC members themselves. In 1991, Saudi Arabia, Qatar and the Arab Emirates joined the US coalition in its blitzkrieg against Iraq. Permanent American military bases were established in these countries in connection with this war, and Kuwait became an American protectorate. OPEC approved UN sanctions against Iraq, which limited it export quotas to a minimum. The world supply of oil did not suffer as a result, since Saudi Arabia and other OPEC members had reserve capacity, and they increased their own quotas for production and export. The founding Arab members of OPEC came under the strategic and political control of the United States and fulfilled US requests for increases in the export of oil. Naturally, world prices for oil began to fall, to 20, 15 and, in 1998, to 10 dollars a barrel. Oil producers outside OPEC, including Russia, Mexico and Britain, whose production prices fluctuated between 11 and 14 dollars a barrel, suffered losses and were displaced from the world market. In the United States, conversely, there began an economic boom, and the growth in the economy coincided with the two terms of President Bill Clinton. This boom, of course, sharpened the appetite for consuming oil. The domestic production of oil in the United States continued to decline. The production of oil from Alaska cost about 15 dollars a barrel. By 2000, the proportion of imported oil in the US economy was approaching 60 per cent. At the same time, the OPEC countries had almost exhausted their existing oil production capacities and could not increase oil exports without capital investment to establish new oil fields. To increase exports in this way would demand much time and capital.

Sanctions or war?

The military operation 'Desert Storm', to free Kuwait of the occupying Iraqi army, stopped unexpectedly on 28 February 1991, on the road to Basra, where it had already led to an uprising of the Arab Shiites against Saddam Hussein. Iraq's regular army was destroyed in the first battle, but the elite forces and the presidential guard remained untouched and were deployed to defend the cities and oil production facilities. Now Saddam could use these forces to put down the uprising of the Shiites in the South and the Kurds in the North. The US leadership and command of the Anti-Iraq coalition, comprising 31 countries, declared a victory which still had not actually been achieved. But for many reasons which it is not essential to go into here, it was decided to finish the war without storming Baghdad, but with strict economic sanctions approved by the United Nations. The idea of the authors of this plan was that Iraq, formerly a developed, enlightened and multi-ethnic country, could not withstand a political and economic blockade which condemned her people to poverty and food rationing. An uprising or coup in Baghdad was expected in two or three years, undoubtedly, not without help from outside.

Iraq actually was a rich country, primarily thanks to her oil. In 1989, the output of oil in Iraq reached one billion barrels a year, of which only 177 million barrels were for internal consumption. Oil production was nationalised in 1971, and the profits from exports, more than ten billion dollars a year, boosted the budget. Iraq had intensive, irrigated land use, horticulture and developed cattle breeding dependent, however, on imported corn. In 1990, gross national product was 73 billion dollars, or 4,110 dollars per capita. This was four times higher than in neighbouring Syria, and twice as high as Turkey.

The introduction, in 1991, of a regime of economic sanctions allowed Iraq to export oil only in exchange for food. This accounted for 100 to 200 million barrels a year, but quotas were set each month and depended on fluctuations in the export price of oil. By 1994, oil exports were worth only 400 million dollars to the country's budget. The sanctions regime actually destroyed the economy of Iraq rather quickly. By 1999, gross national product had fallen to 19 billion dollars, or 850 dollars per capita. Industry and agriculture were in decline. The army could not purchase new equipment. The population subsisted on the physiological minimum, suffering sharp deficits in the rations of livestock products. Every one had 2,446 calories a day. This was just one per cent higher than the United Nations recommended minimum. It was surprising, however, that in these conditions male average life expectancy increased by five years, the birth rate rose, and the population increased from 18 to 24 million. There was no coup. Saddam's regime grew even stronger, since the majority of the dictator's opponents went abroad to western countries, establishing oppositional groups in the United States, Britain or France. In 2001, regular flights from Baghdad to the capitals of neighbouring countries were re-established, and the rail link with Turkey re-opened. Food rations were increased. By mid-2002, eleven years after sanctions were introduced, patience was exhausted, not in Baghdad, but in Washington. Iraq could withstand sanctions for a long time yet. But America could not wait any longer.

Translated by Tony Simpson

Christopher Hill – A Man with a Mission

V. G. Kiernan

V.G. Kiernan, the celebrated historian of imperialism, remembers Christopher Hill, the doyen of British socialist historians.

I first met Christopher Hill in London in a big upstairs room of a not very elegant restaurant, now I believe disappeared, called the 'Garibaldi', a name commemorating the hero's visit to England. It was a warm, sunny day of 1946, and Christopher, in shirt-sleeves, was seated in the middle of one side of a long table. He had, in those days, a quite pronounced stammer, which gradually faded. He was going into some question about the Revolution of 1640. There was no dissent, and it appeared that the 17th century section of the Communist Party's Historians' Group had already fully explored the matter, and reached agreement. To me the conclusions reached were novel, and struck me as unconvincing. I had no real right to butt in, having been away for years in India. I did venture to object, and the outcome was a long-drawn controversy, which ended with my feeling obliged to withdraw my argument, which had left me in a minority of one.

In retrospect I think we were both in some ways wrong. Years later, when Christopher dedicated to me a volume of his collected essays, he credited me with talents including 'wit', not a gift he aspired much to himself. By then he could acknowledge that everyone who had struggled with the Revolution had fallen into miscalculations of some kind, and that in history there is always something more to be explained. None the less, he was piling up from year to year a prodigious quantity of historical explaining.

He was born at York in 1912, his father a solicitor, both his parents Methodists; the Nonconformist enlightenment, of which we both inherited a share, was still not exhausted. He once remarked to me drily that he has been sent to a certain school 'to be turned into a gentleman', and I have wondered whether this had anything to do with his stammer. His early mentor as a Marxist historian was Dona Torr, from another religious background as the daughter of a canon of Chester Cathedral. He got to grips with the Soviet Union by spending a year there and learning Russian; he did this, he told me, chiefly by conning the speeches of Stalin, which contained a few linguistic puzzles.

Dona Torr was a believer in strict adherence to Party rules, and when Christopher became a Party member he may have taken this over from her. Meetings of the historians had for some time been open to all; but he was one of those who insisted on everyone proving himself a bona fide member by showing his Party card, fully stamped up. Anyone eating a restaurant meal ought, he felt, to make an equivalent contribution to the always hard up *Daily Worker*. It had been customary for travel expenses of those attending the historians' meetings to be pooled and divided equally. When some members wanted to give up this socialist principle, he was firm on keeping it up. With all his sterling qualities, it was not easy to feel that one was getting to know him well. He could be genial enough when the occasion warranted it, but any wastage of useful time was not to be thought of. E.P.Thompson once surprised me by saying 'I'm afraid of him', but I could understand the feeling. Christopher was a man with a mission, which demanded some Puritan austerity.

His first marriage demanded some breakaway, beginning, as he confessed, with a scene *in flagrante delicto*. The lady was small, dark-haired, vivacious, and smoked cigarettes, which he never did. It may have been a case of the attraction of opposites. It soon ended, however, and in 1956 his second, permanent marriage took place. Bridget Hill gave the impression of a practical business-like mind. She had been teaching, and was interested in history, and became a college bursar. They stayed with me once in Edinburgh, to escape the thought of a daughter killed in a car accident. One day we had a long walk over the Pentland Hills and lunch at the old Alan Ramsay hotel. At my own rather rough and ready table Bridget tactfully took over the cooking. I visited them in a cottage they had at one time, not far from Oxford, and we tramped energetically through the thick clay soil.

The Party was still small and declining from its wartime peak, and solidarity was a prime virtue; policy directives from the leadership were to be accepted because it could be assumed that they came from Moscow. But an opposite feeling was growing on more and more minds that such directives were not infallible, or might not be well adapted to the British climate. More democracy, more freedom of speech, might be needed. At last, a committee including Hill was appointed to review these questions. It was given much greater impetus by the Soviet military occupation of Hungary, one of the vassal states of Eastern Europe. A large proportion – in Edinburgh, half – of the membership resigned. Hill and others on the committee produced a minority report calling for reform. In 1957 he resigned (in 1959, finding no signs of improvement, I did the same).

When I next met him he said gloomily that he and Bridget were living now in a political vacuum. The Labour Party was not to be thought of as an alternative. Most unexpectedly, the gap was filled by his becoming, in 1965, Master of his College, Balliol. He agreed to stand for election, he told me, on the understanding that he would be left enough free time for writing; and he did go on writing book after book, always in his chosen field of 17th century England.

A Master of late Victorian times, Benjamin Jowett, had turned Balliol into a *serious* place, chiefly in order to supply the empire with reliable administrators. The Master's lodge needed renovation; Christopher did not bother with this, but continued to live outside in his own house. A professor I met at Balliol, who was only there because his Chair was attached to the College, lamented that it was a 'penitential' abode, bereft of social jollity. Christopher was concerned with weightier matters. He wanted to have the college opened to girl students, and he wanted to open its doors to more students lacking the Oxford label of 'effortless superiority'. He even brought some undergraduates onto the college council, remembering perhaps how he had been baulked of something similar in the Party.

He was Master until 1978, and must have found his dozen years of it a strain. He left Oxford, whether or not by way of shaking its dust off his feet, and sought peace and quiet – not idle leisure – in an old township called Sibford Ferris, near Banbury. My last meeting with him – and thanks a good deal to my wife being with us, the happiest – came about when he was asked by some Oxford association to give a talk on the 'English Revolution'. I too was invited to say something, and amused him and the audience with an allusion to our old controversy.

My wife had driven me to Oxford; we were invited to stay the night at Sibford Ferris, and Bridget drove us all there. After some thirty cups of tea Christopher brought up, a little to my surprise, the topic of sloe-gin. He had been learning, as a hobby, to make his own, and brought out two different sorts for us to taste. He added that he and Bridget liked to drink red wine of an evening. Was this a needed protection against the Methodist legacy of over-seriousness? We were then conveyed to Banbury and a lengthy convivial dinner, with a good allowance of the gifts of Bacchus. Bridget drank little, and deposited us safely at their door; Christopher and my wife, however, both stumbled out of the car into a dry ditch beside the road, and I was, for a moment, unsure of my footing.

In the morning we were taken for a windy walk round the neighbourhood, and then for a car ride to where we could catch a bus back to Oxford. On the way, Christopher related a ludicrous story about his undertaking to complete the splendid book on the Levellers that H. N. Brailsford was still busy with when he died. Unluckily, the author's widow was a believer in the spirit world, and at night she would get in touch with her deceased husband and receive his instructions for the next pages of his book, which she handed on to Christopher, to his considerable embarrassment.

My last letter to him was a request for help with an entry in the *Dictionary of National Biography* on his old friend Dona Torr. It was unanswered, until Bridget wrote to tell me of his mental collapse. Perhaps he had at last overloaded his inexhaustible memory; but it was she who was to die first, perhaps from the shock. He followed on February 23.

I happened to be in Los Angeles, where I was meeting Eric Hobsbawm and others who knew Christopher, some years before his death. Several of us were together when news came of his being awarded the Biography prize for his book on Bunyan. I scribbled a congratulation on a postcard, and we all signed it. I had once argued to Christopher that Bunyan must have been a man morbidly self-absorbed. He disagreed, and showed a strong sympathy with Bunyan and his rugged life. Perhaps he was comparing the Pilgrim's progress with his own arduous journey through life, and the failure of so much that he had hoped to see.

War No More
Eliminating Conflict in the Nuclear Age
Robert Hinde and Joseph Rotblat
Foreword by Robert S. McNamara

Never before have so many people worried about the effects of military conflict. At a time when terrorism is opening the way for new forms of warfare worldwide, this book provides a much-needed account of the real dangers we face, and argues that the elimination of weapons of mass destruction and of war are attainable and necessary goals. Written by Nobel Peace prize-winner and former nuclear physicist Joseph Rotbalt, and distinguished scholar Robert Hinde, War No More provides expert insight into the nature of modern warfare and shows how a peaceful future is possible.

August 2003   £10.99 - ISBN 0 7453 2191 7

THE BERTRAND RUSSELL PEACE FOUNDATION
PEACE DOSSIER

'WARMONGERS SELL WAR'

Published in the Financial Times, 10 July 2003
From Sir Rodric Braithwaite
Former head of the Joint Intelligence Committee
London EC2P 2AX

Sir,
If the current row rumbles on, demands for a judicial inquiry into the government's handling of intelligence on Iraq will doubtless grow (report, July 9). Meanwhile, there is little point in speculating on what an inquiry might turn up or its likely effects on the prime minister's fortunes.

But the campaign to win round a sceptical public was not conducted primarily on the basis of intelligence dossiers. In the first months of this year we were bombarded with warnings that British cities might at any moment face a massive terrorist attack. Housewives were officially advised to lay in stocks of food and water. Tanks were sent to Heathrow. People were unwilling to go to war to uphold the authority of the United Nations, to overthrow an evil dictator in a distant country, or to promote democracy throughout the Middle East. But in this atmosphere of near hysteria, they began to believe that Britain itself was under imminent threat and that we should get our blow in first. And so the prime minister managed – just – to swing parliament behind him.

What has happened since then? No weapons of mass destruction have been found. If they exist, they were so deeply hidden as to constitute no imminent threat to Britain. Official warnings of terrorist attacks on our cities have died away, though the incentives for terrorists to attack us have probably been increased, not diminished, by the outcome of the war. Democracy seems as far off as ever from the troubled streets of Baghdad. All may yet be well. At present it does not much look like it.

Fishmongers sell fish; warmongers sell war. Both may sincerely believe in their product. The prime minister surely acted in the best of faith. But it does look as though he seriously oversold his wares. The final judgment will be delivered not by the mandarins, the judges, or the politicians. It will be delivered by the consumer – the British public.

PARTHENON MARBLES

Mrs Marianna V. Vardinoyannis, UNESCO Goodwill Ambassador, has published a graphic brochure showing what the Parthenon would look like if re-united with the so-called 'Elgin' Marbles. We circulated this to a number of writers and artists. Among those who have responded are John Arden, Trevor Griffiths and Kurt Vonnegut. This is the response of Ralph Steadman, the artist.

Never has there been a more appropriate time to begin to redress the imbalance of history. The British Government could generate, in one magnanimous gesture, a chain of events that would show the world that sanity is reborn, and the 21st century is, indeed, the new age of enlightenment.

They could return the Parthenon Marbles to their rightful home on the hill of the Acropolis in Athens, and lay to rest one of the most notorious acts of vandalism ever perpetrated from behind a curtain of colonial democracy, political mendacity and personal vanity.

Ironically, on the Marbles themselves, are depictions of wars being fought. Olympian Gods are fighting giants, Greeks are battling the Amazons, men are fighting centaurs and Troy is falling. All is war. All is marble. It predates the Bayeux Tapestry by nearly 2000 years, but tells the same story: one is hewn; one is embroidered. Both are miracles. That any of the Parthenon stands at all is a miracle. In its long history it has been both a Christian Church and an Islamic Mosque with a Minaret on top. The Goths sacked most cities, but spared Athens. The Crusaders trashed Constantinople, but chose Athens as their centre of operations, transforming the Parthenon into the Roman Catholic Church of Notre Dame. It has served as shelter for the wretched, and iconic totem for beliefs of permanence through the ages. The Turks used it as a gunpowder arsenal in the 17th century until the Venetians blew the roof off, destroying the sculptured statues and sections of the pediments and their columns. They left the Parthenon a virtual ruin, leaving behind piles of powdered marble and beautifully sculpted building blocks, plundered mercilessly later to rebuild elsewhere. Even the lead core between the column sections was melted out and re-used to make bullets.

Early tourists of the 18th century from Western Europe were buying fragments of its sculptures and pediments, transporting them back home to adorn gardens of stately homes and fishponds of the rich and rancid dross of the burgeoning Empire. Nevertheless, what is left stands as proud as ever, an icon of classical antiquity, and the cornerstone symbol of democracy. It is acknowledged as an architectural vision of perfection, of austerity and grace.

The Parthenon was built to honour Athena, a Greek Goddess, in the 5th century B.C., and it housed, among other breathtaking examples of naïve, pure genius, her gold and marble statue. Athena was one of the daughters of Zeus, a virgin Goddess (but who would want Zeus for a father-in-law?), a storm and lightening Goddess, no less, (Athene means 'to strike' in Greek), and a patron of the Arts of

Peace and prudent intelligence; moisture being her main attribute, which seems odd. I cannot figure out what that means, but with a little more research, maybe I could.

Then the final irony; along comes Thomas, 7th Earl of Elgin, 11th Earl of Kincardine, in 1799, a 29 year old Scottish career diplomat, wishing to build a vulgar mansion for his wealthy young bride as a wedding present. It was to be called Broom Hall.

Persuaded by a hired architect, Harrison, also a Thomas, who should have known better, Elgin used his influence as the new Ambassador to Constantinople – a 'sultanate' in residence to those who cracked whips like gods themselves – to gain unlimited access to crawl all over the Ottoman empire, wherever his heart desired, and have detailed drawings and plaster casts made of absolutely anything, which included what was left of the Parthenon, and which still included the Marbles – the enigmatic relief Frieze of sublime enticement.

I believe that the Marbles proved too much of a temptation for this ambitious, lovelorn young man. Why merely draw them or bother to cast them, for that matter, when you can simply take them – with a spot of heavy lifting? Labour was dirt cheap. Authority was feared with life-threatening intensity, so its power flourished unquestionably. I might have felt the same myself at the time – in the same position, and with the same ridiculous aspirations. It was an avaricious accident waiting to happen. After all, most of the rest had been blown to bits or fallen down, anyway. So who cares? No one then, that's for sure, except for a few scholars, who would disappear conveniently, in the blessed mists of time. The unlearned lesson of history is forever present.

So, Elgin employed 300 local musclemen for a year, to tear down the Parthenon Marbles and ship them to Scotland to adorn his 'classical' spread and impress the Society of Dilettanti, an exclusive club of erudite zealots, who were as much of a spur to his blind ambition as his wife must have been. 200 crates containing some of civilisation's most unbearably beautiful pieces of sculptured marble were shipped back to Scotland for nothing. At that time, and even now, high-flying diplomats can move murder victims around the world without an export license in the name of national security. Meanwhile, his wife had left him for another. But that was after he had spent five years in a French jail. He returned to Scotland in 1806 to find a hellish *brouhaha* surrounding the action he had taken all those years ago.

An archaeologist, Richard Payne Knight, attacked Elgin – more, I suspect, in a fit of jealousy than because of altruistic moral fervour. Nobody is perfect. Lord Elgin had cornered the best, the highest, the most enlightened work of Greek intelligence and esoteric perfection. Perversely, he may have inadvertently saved them from subsequent destruction. We will never know. Displayed in London, the works, even in their broken form, showed artists and experts alike the art of the impossible. Lord Elgin was vilified, but it did not prevent the British Government from doling out £72,000 for the collection of fragments (putting Lord Elgin £35,000 in front after total expenses), which were then housed, with due ceremony by the great and the good, in the British Museum. Official plunder, displayed officially for all to gloat over.

Nobody batted an eyelid. The 'Elgin'Marbles belonged to England, like most other things upon which the sun never set, at the time.

Times change. And now we, as benefactors (inheritors?) of a scum-laden past, must square our collective conscience irrespective of whether others do it. That is not the point.

The point is, we have an opportunity to lead the way. We have an opportunity to demonstrate our fabled reputation for fair play. We have this definitive chance to say, 'We must beg your forgiveness for past transgressions'. We must show humility. Redressed actions. No one need lose face. The wrongs are long gone, but the damage done hovers like a drip in a damp cave.

A perfect copy of the Parthenon Marbles is within our power to have, and a perfect copy is all we need. And then we say, 'Citizens of Greece! Please accept, with our deepest apologies, and in the name of peace and democracy, your Parthenon Marbles'.

DEPLETED URANIUM

How not to deal with nuclear waste? Christopher Gifford asks 'how did plutonium find its way to Kosovo?'

Depleted uranium was first described as mainly the isotope Uranium 238. To make reactor fuel or an atomic bomb natural uranium has to be enriched by increasing the proportion of the isotope uranium 235 from 0.7% to more than 2%. The uranium 235 then will support a chain reaction with the release of much energy. The uranium metal from which the fissile isotope 235 has been extracted to make fuel for Magnox reactors is called depleted uranium.

Depleted uranium (DU) has a density 1.7 times that of lead. It is toxic as well as being mildly radioactive with a half-life of 4.5 billion years. In spite of the toxicity and the ability to cause cancer and genetic mutations the military found it useful to increase the penetrating power of shells and bullets and even to improve the armour on military vehicles. DU munitions were test fired in Britain and the United States in the 1980s and used in Iraq in 1991, in Bosnia in 1996, in the Kosovo conflict in 1999, in Afghanistan in 2002, and in Iraq in 2003. It was estimated that the amount of depleted uranium used in the 1991 Gulf war was 340 tonnes. In the 2003 attack on Iraq up to 2000 tonnes may have been used with up to 7 tonnes used in single 'bunker busting' bombs.

Servicemen and women's organisations and others interested in the health of service personnel and civilians questioned the consequences of battlefield exposure to radioactive and toxic materials inhaled as dust or ingested with food.[1] The Ministry of Defence (MoD) response was unequivocal. The risks were negligible except for persons who remained for a long period in a vehicle hit by such a weapon and the MoD denied the contrary findings of its own leaked report as 'a discredited draft prepared by a trainee.'[2] But independent researchers took samples from service personnel indicating the ingestion of 15 times what the MoD had described as a 'safe dose'. Most physicists agree that there is no such thing as a safe dose. Scientists from the United Nations Environment Programme called for recoverable fragments of depleted uranium to be removed from conflict sites. The Royal Society also called for sampling, clean up and monitoring.[3]

In his book *Sixty Years of Nuclear History,* published in 1999, Fred Roberts, a former atom bomb scientist, described depleted uranium also as a product of the reprocessing of spent fuel from nuclear reactors.[4] Within a few months Paul Brown, the environment correspondent of *The Guardian,* after discussions with MoD staff but without attribution, also described depleted uranium as a product of reprocessing.[5] The awful truth was out. The nuclear industry and the MoD had not only found a new way of dealing with mildly radioactive 'natural' nuclear waste. It was helping to dispose of waste from reactors and reprocessing plants which would contain transuranic elements, even allowing for the fact that at least some of the plutonium had been recovered.

Transuranic elements like plutonium are formed in nuclear reactors and are not found in the earth's crust. When the UN environment programme found traces of plutonium and other highly radioactive particles in Kosovo, the Ministry of Defence and the US Department of Energy admitted that the material came from depleted uranium shells but denied that the uranium had been reprocessed. The uranium had been 'accidentally contaminated' in containers containing reprocessed materials.[6] Two months later the UN Environment Programme report on sites in Bosnia referred to 'huge variations' in plutonium levels in pieces of munitions found.

Explanations of 'accidental contamination' became unnecessary in November 2001. The United Kingdom's Environment Agency commissioned and published a report 'Depleted Uranium: a Study of its Uses within the UK and Disposal Issues'[7]. In a general description of depleted uranium the report states in an opening paragraph 'Depleted uranium (DU) is the main by-product of the uranium enrichment process wherein the content of the fissile isotope U235 is enhanced in relation to the U238 content. In addition DU is produced from the reprocessing of Magnox reactor fuel in the UK.' A similar extended definition of depleted uranium appeared in September 2001 when the Department for Environment, Food and Rural Affairs published policy proposals for the management of radioactive waste.[8]

The Environment Agency report estimated worldwide stocks of depleted uranium at well over one million tonnes. The total is estimated to double by 2015. It is by no means the most troublesome of the nuclear industry's waste – plutonium is toxic, highly radioactive and an atomic bomb material. The Secretary of State for Trade and Industry quoted the future cost of managing nuclear waste in the United Kingdom at £85,000,000,000.[9] No safe method of disposal has yet been devised. We can be sure that firing it at one's enemies will not solve the problem either.

The Ministry of Defence justify the use of depleted uranium because to desist from its use would expose British service personnel to greater risks. There is no doubt that guided weapons, satellite technology and the greater penetrating power of bombs and shells were major factors in the military supremacy which led to the rapid defeat of Iraqi forces. But the use of toxic and radioactive materials is a form of chemical and nuclear warfare no different from the use of a radioactive 'dirty bomb' postulated as a possible terrorist weapon. The effects on the environment will last for thousands of years with many generations exposed to genetic effects. International agreement on the prohibition of such weapons and the release of civil nuclear materials for military purposes is needed and the countries best placed to bring that about are the United States and the United Kingdom.

Notes
1. The web site of the Campaign Against Depleted Uranium is http://www.cadu.org.uk. The e-mail address for CADU News is info@cadu.org.uk
2. *The Guardian:* editorial 12.1.01.
3. 'The Health Hazards of Depleted Uranium Munitions: Part 1'. The Royal Society May 2001. Part 2 was published in March 2002.
4. 'Sixty Years of Nuclear History' Fred Roberts 1999 Jon Carpenter Publishing
5. 'Cheap and Lethal Nuclear By-product' Paul Brown *The Guardian* 12.1.01
6. Paul Brown *The Guardian* 18.1.01. He also quoted John Large of Large Associates saying that plutonium was 100 times more dangerous than uranium.
7. The Environment Agency: Technical Report P3-088/TR 27pp with 42 references. November 2001. Alan Martin Associates.
8. 'Managing Radioactive Waste Safely' DEFRA and the Devolved Administrations September 2001. This document had little to say about military use of uranium metal but defined *depleted reprocessed uranium* as a sub-category of depleted uranium. In response to the DEFRA proposals I wrote 'Explanations are now needed on the accuracy with which other transuranic radioactive material is removed from spent fuel before it is released for use as munitions and by whose authority it is released. We are here discussing what to do with nuclear waste and learning, in passing, that firing it at one's enemies is a legitimate method of disposal! Such use should be prohibited by the UK government and by international agreement.'
9. Hansard House of Commons debates for 18 October 2001 Rt Hon Margaret Beckett MP Secretary of State for Trade and Industry.

UN IN THE MELTING POT...

An authoritative voice of the Bush administration is Richard Perle, pioneer of the Project for a New American Century. This was his considered view of the artificially induced crisis in the United Nations after the Security Council rejected the British-American proposal for an attack on Iraq.

Saddam Hussein's reign of terror is about to end. He will go quickly, but not alone: in a parting irony, he will take the UN down with him. Well, not the whole UN. The 'good works' part will survive, the low-risk peacekeeping bureaucracies will remain, the chatterbox on the Hudson will continue to bleat. What will die is the fantasy of the UN as the foundation of a new world order. As we sift the debris, it will be important to preserve, the better to understand, the intellectual wreckage of the liberal conceit of safety through international law administered by international institutions.

As free Iraqis document the quarter-century nightmare of Saddam's rule, let us not forget who held that the moral authority of the international community was enshrined in a plea for more time for inspectors, and who marched against 'regime change'. In the spirit of post-war reconciliation that diplomats are always eager to engender, we must not reconcile the timid, blighted notion that world order requires us to recoil before rogue states that terrorise their own citizens and menace ours.

A few days ago, Shirley Williams argued on television against a coalition of the willing using force to liberate Iraq. Decent, thoughtful and high-minded, she must surely have been moved into opposition by an argument so convincing that it overpowered the obvious moral case for removing Saddam's regime. For Lady Williams (and many others), the thumb on the scale of judgment about this war is the idea that only the UN Security Council can legitimise the use of force. It matters not if troops are used only to enforce the UN's own demands. A willing coalition of liberal democracies isn't good enough. If any institution or coalition other than the UN Security Council uses force, even as a last resort, 'anarchy', rather than international law, would prevail, destroying any hope for world order.

This is a dangerously wrong idea that leads inexorably to handing great moral and even existential politico-military decisions, to the likes of Syria, Cameroon, Angola, Russia, China and France. When challenged with the argument that if a policy is right with the approbation of the security council, how can it be wrong just because communist China or Russia or France or a gaggle of minor dictatorships withhold their assent, she fell back on the primacy of 'order' versus 'anarchy'.

But is the Security Council capable of ensuring order and saving us from anarchy? History suggests not. The UN arose from the ashes of a war that the League of Nations was unable to avert. It was simply not up to confronting Italy in Abyssinia, much less–had it survived that débâcle–to taking on Nazi Germany.

In the heady aftermath of the allied victory, the hope that security could be made collective was embodied in the UN Security Council – with abject results.

During the Cold War the Security Council was hopelessly paralysed. The Soviet empire was wrestled to the ground, and eastern Europe liberated, not by the UN, but by the mother of all coalitions, Nato. Apart from minor skirmishes and sporadic peacekeeping missions, the only case of the security council acting during the Cold War was its use of force to halt the invasion of South Korea–and that was only possible because the Soviets were not in the chamber to veto it. It was a mistake they did not make again.

Facing Milosevic's multiple aggressions, the UN could not stop the Balkan wars or even protect its victims. It took a coalition of the willing to save Bosnia from extinction. And when the war was over, peace was made in Dayton, Ohio, not in the UN. The rescue of Muslims in Kosovo was not a UN action: their cause never gained Security Council approval. The United Kingdom, not the United Nations, saved the Falklands.

This new century now challenges the hopes for a new world order in new ways. We will not defeat or even contain fanatical terror unless we can carry the war to the territories from which it is launched. This will sometimes require that we use force against states that harbour terrorists, as we did in destroying the Taliban regime in Afghanistan.

The most dangerous of these states are those that also possess weapons of mass destruction. Iraq is one, but there are others. Whatever hope there is that they can be persuaded to withdraw support or sanctuary from terrorists rests on the certainty and effectiveness with which they are confronted. The chronic failure of the Security Council to enforce its own resolutions is unmistakable: it is simply not up to the task. We are left with coalitions of the willing. Far from disparaging them as a threat to a new world order, we should recognise that they are, by default, the best hope for that order, and the true alternative to the anarchy of the abject failure of the UN.

... AND NATO AS WELL?

The United States Government is considering organising a Global Peacekeeping Force which would operate outside the purview of the United Nations and NATO, reports Esther Schrader of the Los Angeles Times (27 June 2003).

Defence Secretary Donald H. Rumsfeld is discussing the possibility of the United States organising a standing international peacekeeping force that could be dispatched to trouble spots around the globe. The force would operate outside the auspices of the United Nations and NATO and would include thousands of US Army troops trained for, and permanently assigned to, peacekeeping work. Such an undertaking would represent a major reversal by the Bush administration, which came into office deeply opposed to tying up US military forces in international peacekeeping operations. The plan would probably be opposed by the Army, which has resisted efforts to have its troops drawn into peacekeeping duties.

There are other obstacles as well. Some analysts question how many nations would sign up for such a force if it were under the control of the United States, whose willingness to collaborate with other countries is highly suspect in many parts of the world.

'It seems to me that they have now decided that this is a great opportunity for multilateralism. Who knows, maybe somebody will buy it,' said retired Maj. Gen. William Nash, who commanded a tank division in the 1991 Persian Gulf War and, later, NATO peacekeepers in Bosnia-Herzegovina.

With more than half the Army's deployable troops now engaged in peacekeeping and stabilisation operations around the world, including Bosnia, Kosovo, Afghanistan and especially Iraq, the Pentagon says its purely military capabilities are stretched thin – a problem that is widely acknowledged.

Senior Bush administration officials are coming to believe that the best solution is to create a standing constabulary force made up of troops from a range of countries – but led and trained by the US. It would be distinct from a proposed North Atlantic Treaty Organisation rapid-response force and apart from the United Nations, which has provided peacekeeping missions for decades.

'I am interested in the idea of our leading, or contributing to in some way, a cadre of people in the world who would like to participate in peacekeeping or peacemaking,' Rumsfeld told a group of defence industry leaders at a dinner in Washington last week. 'I think that it would be a good thing if our country provided some leadership for training of other countries' citizens who would like to participate in peacekeeping so that we have a ready cadre of people who are trained and equipped and organised and have communications that they can work with each other.'

The Pentagon has been accused of being unprepared for the post-war violence in Iraq, and Army officials have complained that they are not trained to do the kind of police work that is needed there. 'We're not terribly good at peacekeeping, so I don't know why we would be training people to be peacekeepers,' said Charles Pena, director of defence policy studies at the Cato Institute, a Washington-based think tank.

But a senior defence official said, 'The way Secretary Rumsfeld envisions it, anyone with concerns about US peacekeeping should be assuaged, because the whole idea is for us to do less, rather than more, peacekeeping.'

Though Rumsfeld has defended the military's post-war performance, he acknowledged to a questioner in the dinner audience that it would have been good to have such a force set up before the war. 'It's something that is being discussed in a very serious way by some very serious people right now,' the defence official said, speaking on condition of anonymity.

But the official said Rumsfeld had not decided how many US troops he would recommend allocating to such a force. Nor has the overall size of such a force, or who would pay for it, been addressed. The idea has been broached with unidentified countries in Europe and Latin America, officials said. Other defence officials said the force would probably require about 10,000 US troops.

The notion of creating US military units permanently assigned to peacekeeping was widely discussed at the Pentagon during the Clinton administration, when US forces found themselves increasingly involved in non-military missions in such places as Haiti, Bosnia and Kosovo.

Upon taking office, President Bush promised to pull US peacekeepers out of the Balkans and to launch an immediate review of troop commitments in dozens of countries, with an eye to strictly limiting overseas deployments. But since the September 11 attacks, peacekeeping has come to be viewed by Republicans as more relevant to national security. Indeed, as regards the number of soldiers engaged in peacekeeping, it is the fastest-growing mission of the US military.

'We could take or leave peacekeeping operations in the 1990s – we left Haiti, we left Somalia. The sense was that it might be regrettable in terms of local conditions but not seen as a security threat to the United States,' said Andrew Krepinevich Jr., executive director of the Center for Strategic and Budgetary Assessments, a nonpartisan defense think tank. 'Now failed states are seen as potential breeding grounds for terrorists, and even though we have sizable forces already engaged in peacekeeping operations, there may be more to come.'

Defence officials say Rumsfeld's proposal is consistent with the aim of limiting US overseas deployments. Though it would professionalise a small number of American troops in peacekeeping, it would aim to enlist other countries to contribute the vast majority of troops to such a force, with the promise that they would be trained and organised by the United States.

The United States has about 5,500 peacekeeping troops in Bosnia, Kosovo, Macedonia, Croatia and the Sinai peninsula, in addition to the 150,000-plus presence in Afghanistan and Iraq. None of the troops are peacekeepers by vocation, and not all receive such training before deploying. Still, as envisioned, creating a standing international peacekeeping force that is US-led or -trained would allow the Pentagon to exert considerably more control over peacekeeping than in the past.

The United Nations has historically organised such missions. Though the United States foots 27% of the bill for UN peacekeeping, it doesn't control the missions. It hasn't provided significant forces since the 1993 mission in Somalia.

After the months of bitter division over how to confront Iraq, many United Nations Security Council members aren't inclined to help the United States keep the peace in that country, a UN official said. Nor is Washington inclined to ask, after having failed to win UN backing for its plans – along with Britain and other members of a coalition – to invade Iraq.

'No one is talking about UN peacekeepers' for Iraq, said a US diplomat.

At the Pentagon, defence officials said that although Rumsfeld has broached his idea in meetings recently with senior Army officials, he has not ordered a formal study or set a timetable for implementation. But 'it's really a timely problem and, moving forward, it's really important to ask, 'Is there a different way to configure this?' one official said. 'Everybody sort of thinks there is.'

Army leaders historically have been sceptical of turning any of their professional fighters into professional peacekeepers, and have publicly opposed such plans. In recent years, the US role in Bosnia, Kosovo, Macedonia and Croatia has become primarily the province of the National Guard and the reserves. 'In their heart of hearts, they feel very strongly that they don't want to be peacekeepers, and who can blame them, because war fighting is what they do, and we need to be very careful before we have them not doing that,' said Nash, the retired general. 'Armies see themselves when they get up in the morning as war fighters. When you get the Army doing lots of other things, you have a bad army.'

Said a current Army official: 'Is there any unit of the U.S. Army that wants to be "Peacekeepers-R-Us?" Not exactly.'

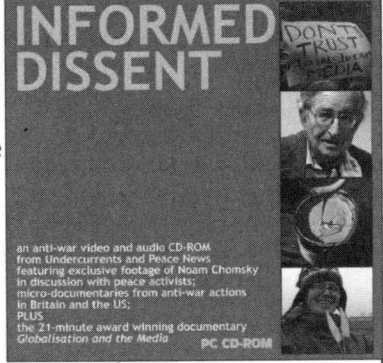

INFORMED DISSENT

A new *Peace News* and *Undercurrents* anti-war video CD-ROM featuring:
Exclusive footage of Noam Chomsky in discussion with peace activists, micro-documentaries from anti-war actions in Britain and the US
PLUS award winning *Undercurrents* documentary *Globalisation and the Media*.
Price: £6.50. Buy your copy online now by visiting **www.peacenews.info** or send a cheque made out to "Peace News" to: 5 Caledonian Rd, London N1 9DY.

Also **coming soon: Peace News** 2451 on North East Asia, examining radical social movements and nonviolent activism in China, Taiwan, North and South Korea and Hong Kong. Including contributions from Korean Women's Network Against Militarism and *Tokyo Progressive*. Ask your local retailer to order your copy. For subscription details call 020 7278 3344 or visit the webshop.

Reviews

Whither Eurasia?

Vassilis K. Fouskas, *Zones of Conflict*, Pluto Press, 177 pages, hardback ISBN 0 74532 030 9 £45, paperback ISBN 0 74532 029 5 £14.99

This most interesting book is an extended discussion of the thesis of Zbigniew Brzezinski in *The Grand Chessboard*. Fouskas begins by taking Brzezinski's text as his theme: 'Eurasia has been the centre of world power' ever since the continents began to interact politically.

> 'Russia, Austro-Hungary, France, the Ottoman Empire, Britain and Germany all wanted to dominate this bizarre landscape ranging from the French shores of the Atlantic down to the Persian Gulf, and from the Chinese land mass to Central Asia, the Black Sea, the Turkish Straits and the Suez. Brzezinski observes that all of the powers claiming mastery over Eurasia in the past were part of its landscape, but now "for the first time ever, a non Eurasian power has emerged not only as the key arbiter of Eurasian power relations, but also as the world's paramount power".'

Brzezinski's is now the voice of an older generation of American strategists. He very much supported the enlargement of Europe, because it would 'expand the range of American influence'. But he was firmly committed against the 'deepening of European social and political integration', seeing this as a straightforward challenge to American supremacy. He was very much in favour of the enlargement of Nato, as a device for extending military influence and American hegemony over wider areas, including the former Communist world. Initially famous as the voice of 'human rights', he was reproached with inconsistency upon the publication of *The Grand Chessboard*, because the book was stiff with *realpolitik*. There was no contradiction, he replied to critics.

> 'I elaborated that doctrine (of human rights) in agreement with President Carter, as it was the best way to destabilize the Soviet Union. And it worked.'

Well, perhaps it worked once. Will it work again? This is the rueful question which may well be asked about the world's new police force against weapons of mass destruction. This may well find the next and subsequent military actions progressively more difficult to undertake than the earlier, and no American administration will readily find acceptance of its agenda for human rights in the aftermath of the concentration camp at Guantanamo Bay, and Mr. Brzezinski's candid admission.

Nato stratagems have also been wearing thin. Once the new post-jubilee Nato had undertaken its first direct military engagement, in Kosovo, the American forces began to find this brilliant engine of dominance had its downside. Nato was, after all, an alliance, governed by a Council of its Member-states, even if these might be bypassed much of the time. There was no way in which they could conduct a war without meeting. And as soon as they met, they disagreed. There were different priorities, different military polices, different personalities, and different national interests. Before the end of the Kosovo confrontation, key American generals were, if not eating the rugs on HQ floors, at any rate strongly moved to promise themselves 'never again!' Bombing policy, targeting, military planning, all became objects of contention, frustration and ultimately, rage.

So cauterizing was this experience to prove, that no attempt was made to mobilise Nato after the attack of 9/11 once the invasion of Afghanistan had been fixed upon. Now the preferred formula for military alliance was to be the 'alliance of the willing', in which all the orders could be given by Americans, and subordinate powers could be co-ordinated, or perhaps dropped, at will. Since then, willing though they may have been, Nato has not been invited to join the occupation of Iraq, even though some Member-states were almost pathetically anxious so to do.

The modern American alliance is of those willing to abandon any pretension to lead or determine their own polices. The numbers of the willing are therefore likely to shrink over time.

All these developments have been sharpening up since Fouskas completed this text: but he could already see some of the tensions which were afflicting Brzezinski's model.

Military power is not enough, even for the most powerful military in the world. Fouskas tells this as it is:

> 'America's military might and global reach notwithstanding, it can never violently confront a politically united Europe/Eurasia, for American national identity does not really function as a unifying element of America's social order. In the main, America's modernity is a by-product of Eurasia, that is to say, of its ethnic identities and industrious peoples.
>
> Despite the shortcomings of the European Enlightenment and the regressive/divisive aspects of Europe's nationalisms...national identities across Europe are so well embedded that they need no further artificial boost from their political élite. If a concerted effort were made to advance notions of European citizenship and European social and political order, then Europe's national identities could coexist peacefully, projecting an image of fraternity, solidarity and social justice.'

The emerging unity of Europe, for Fouskas, affords a bridge in ethnic and cultural pluralism, across which the other America, based on American pluralism, can be reached. The implosion of the third way at the end of the '90s has left space for a new democratic alliance, which can reach from Europe out to Russia and China, and seek to shape a new Eurasia, able to assert its own values, and ultimately transform America.

Ken Coates

'Utopians'

John Platts-Mills, QC, *Muck, Silk and Socialism: Reflections of a Left-wing Queen's Council,* **Paper Publishing, Oldwood Cottage, Wedmore, Somerset, BS28 4XW, 687 pages, hardback ISBN 0 95399 490 2 £28**

Archie Potts, *Zilliacus: a Life for Peace and Socialism,* **Merlin Press, 227 pages, paperback ISBN 0 85036 509 0 £14.95**

Denis Healey, whilst still head of the Labour Party's International Department, summed up how he saw the thinking of the 'Old Labour' of his day.

> 'Much of the Party still took a utopian view of world politics. Many at every level of the movement still had their pre-war illusions about Stalin's Russia as the workers' paradise. An even larger number distrusted the United States. Above all, there was general reluctance to accept that the defeat of Hitler and Mussolini had not in itself created the conditions for a lasting peace. With so much to do at home, the idea of continuing to direct resources to defence was universally unwelcome.'

These two books celebrate the lives of two of the foremost 'utopians', who perpetually tested the patience of Ernest Bevin, Healey's mentor, and were to become a byword for fellow-travelling. In fact, both men were expelled from the Labour Party, alongside three other Labour MPs, as the new Cold War began to take wings. Widely denounced as 'crypto-Communists', they were invested by their opponents with a fictitious uniformity of views, which quickly unravels if one reads these two most interesting books.

Zilliacus was a pioneer of the League of Nations, and a genuine expert on international affairs. Platts-Mills worked for sixty years as a barrister, and conducted a number of high profile cases. His book is nothing if not readable. It follows his migration from New Zealand to Oxford, and the beginning of his friendship with the Czechoslovak refugee, Otto Sling, when both were working in London in various anti-fascist causes. With the outbreak of war, after some remarkable political adventures, he found himself working in the mines as a Bevin boy in Doncaster. From there he became a member of the post-war House of Commons, part of the great influx of Labour Members which found him sitting alongside Zilliacus in 1945.

Platts-Mills is nothing if not candid. 'I must have been world Stalin lover number one' he wrote.

> 'When Khrushchev denounced him in February 1956, I still would not accept it. I reasoned "if there is a conspiracy in Moscow this is it: a conspiracy to rob Stalin of his just fame as a saviour of the world from the Nazis".'

But at last the penny dropped. His old friend Otto Sling had been murdered in 1952, after a dreadful mock trial in which Zilliacus himself had been cited as an agent of British Intelligence.

Zilliacus, if not world Stalin lover number two, had earned an unjustified reputation for putting the telescope to his blind eye when approaching all things Soviet; but this was abruptly dashed when Stalin expelled Yugoslavia from the family of Communist States, and Tito was anathematised as a Fascist and arch traitor. Zilliacus not only defended Tito, but campaigned on behalf of the Yugoslav Communists who had been so gravely traduced. By this time he was unacceptable to official Labour, and 'Titoism' made him anathema to official Communists. He was to receive a bitter lesson from the Slansky trial in which Otto Sling was sentenced to death, because this was but the latest judicial scandal in a series of monstrous frame-ups which had begun with the Moscow trials of the late 1930s, which hitherto had always been defended by Zilliacus himself and his co-thinkers.

These books could be taken as extended apologias for two victims of an elaborate con-trick, or they could be seen as confessions of the gullible. But actually, they are much more interesting than that: they record the lives of two clever and idealistic people, who truly dedicated their lives to human betterment. It is difficult, even for the most agnostic and sceptical among us, to fail to find some common ground with two such men, who, when they were wrong, were spectacularly wrong, but when they were right gave us, more than once, new examples in courage and steadfastness.

G.Allen

Unethical Foreign Policy

Mark Curtis, *Web of Deceit: Britain's Real Role in the World*, Vintage, paperback ISBN 0 09944 839 4 £7.99

In January 2002, our Prime Minister visited India. According to Downing Street, the main purpose of this visit was to address industrialists, with the obligatory courtesy meetings with his Indian equivalents. His speech went mainly unreported, but shortly after these meetings I discovered a story on the BBC's World Service Urdu web site. It ran that the Indian defence minister George Fernandes disclosed that the issue of India acquiring Advanced Jet Trainers was raised by British Prime Minister Tony Blair with Prime Minister A B Vajpayee. These, of course, are the same jet trainers Britain sold to Indonesia as BAE Hawk jets, and under which could be slung all sorts of offensive anti-personnel munitions. All this took place at a time when India and Pakistan, two nuclear armed states, were in a stand-off over Kashmir.

Tony Blair's trip to India was to hustle for a billion pound arms deal from a developing country. So, what's new?

Mark Curtis's book *Web of Deceit, Britain's Real Role in the World* provides us with a level of detail and reference to sources relentlessly gathered together from reports and official government material which disclose the theme running through British foreign policy since 1945. The theme certainly is not that proclaimed by New Labour, of being 'a force for good in the world'. New Labour has so distorted the English language that humanitarian intervention is understood by its recipients as the darkening of the skies above their wretched countries as the B52s fly over and drop their cargoes which most assuredly put thousands instantly out of their misery, but create a living hell of powerlessness and fear for those remaining.

It is the links between the political élites, the merchants of death and the defence of world capitalism that Curtis so well establishes. Old Labour and its complicity in the downfall of Mossadeq in Iran in support of the activities of the Anglo-Iranian Oil Company, now BP and referred to by satirists as Blair Petroleum, through to the Iraq of today. How can you argue on the one hand that your intervention in Kosovo is humanitarian, and yet state as Blair did that 'we will carry on pounding day after day after day, until our objectives are secured.' And what were these objectives? It turns out that the peace settlement at the end of the campaign was exactly that proposed by the Serbian National Assembly at Rambouillet before the start of the bombing.

Mark Curtis quotes from government documents which add greatly to his work because of the chatty, clubbable nature of one foreign office mandarin speaking to another. In Indonesia, where our record requires criminal investigation, Curtis quotes our man in Jakarta, Sir Andrew Gilchrist, in a cosy memo to the Foreign Office: 'I have never concealed from you my belief that a little shooting in Indonesia would be an essential preliminary to effective change.' I later met the said Sir Andrew in the Scottish town of Lanark. He was standing on a wooden platform, in full highland dress, taking the salute at the World Pipe Band Championships. By then he was out of diplomacy but into quangos as the Chairman of the Highlands and Islands Development Board, placed there by Ted Heath no doubt for services rendered. Fortunately for our highland peoples the establishment no longer had the services of the Duke of Cumberland.

Henry McCubbin

Amicus fighting for the liberty of working people at home and abroad

Joint General Secretary
Derek Simpson

Joint General Secretary
Roger Lyons